MAKING
MEMORY
BO

BOX PROJECTS T

BARBA

First published in the United States of America by
Rockport Publishers, Inc.
33 Commercial Street
Gloucester, Massachusetts 01930-5089
Telephone: (978) 282-9590
Facsimile: (978) 283-2742
www.rockpub.com

ISBN 1-56496-711-5

10 9 8 7 6 5 4 3 2 1

Design: Lynn Faitelson

Printed in China.

contents

introduction

Anyone who has ever filled a shoe box with family photos or crammed small treasures into a cigar box has already made a memory box. Without having quite defined it before, we know exactly what it is. We also know that as we go through life squirreling away letters, seashells, report cards, broken watches, snippets of baby hair, and all of the ephemera of belonging, these boxes contain the core of a life. This book will teach you how to make the container as special as its contents.

However varied their design, most boxes share basic architectural elements. A case, a tray, a lid, and a flap—four units, and at least four hundred ways to multiply, divide, and join them to create unique objects of beauty, whimsy, and practicality. The Postcard Box is no more than an extended case. The Jewelry Box is a tray mounted on a case. The Candy Box is simply two nesting trays. If you visually break down each of these boxes, identifying the components, you will see how finite are the parts—and how infinite the decorative possibilities.

And that is how I would begin—by looking at the pictures. Undress the boxes and get down to the bones. Notice differences. Compare similarities. The Patchwork Box and The Artist's Portfolio seem worlds apart, yet both consist of cases with separately constructed flaps. The configuration of the cases and the placement and shape of the flaps vary, but the skeleton is the same.

Here is the heartening fact about boxmaking: Boxes do not become more difficult as you proceed from one style to another; they simply become either more like or less like each other. By the time you have completed one of each component—a tray, a case, a lid, and a flap—you will know all there is to know about the fundamentals of boxmaking. Then you can start to have fun.

The most important part of this book is the chapter on The Basics. Keep a bookmark in place: You will refer to this chapter often because it contains all of the technical details necessary to construct boxes. Don't cut a single sheet of paper before reading How to Measure. Don't dip your brush into a glue bowl until the discussion on adhesives makes sense to you.

The personality of a box is in the heart and hands of its maker and in its materials. Surround yourself with your paper treasures, open that shoe box filled with family photos, get out your tools, and go to work.

the essentials: *tools*

The following tools are essential to making memory boxes:

AWL: A wooden-handled tool with a sharp, pointy metal shaft, used to punch holes; from bookbinding suppliers and hardware stores.

BRUSHES: For gluing: ¹/₂" (1 cm) and 2" (5 cm) wide short-handled flat brushes (cheap) from the hardware store.
For pasting: 1¹/₂" round natural-bristle brushes (expensive but should last a lifetime) from Italy and France. Check out pastry brushes in cookware stores or go to your bookbinding supplier.

C-CLAMPS: A hardware store item, used to clamp boards to the workbench, to stabilize box parts as they are being glued.

CHISEL: Wood chisels from the hardware store, in a variety of sizes (to match the width of ribbons used as box closures).

CUTTING MAT: A self-healing mat board, imprinted with a grid pattern, on which endless cuts can be made with your knives; available in several sizes from bookbinding and art supply stores.

DRILL: A drill with small drill bits, to pierce holes in wood and plastic elements.

FOLDERS, BONE AND TEFLON: Folders are used to fold and crease paper, to turn materials over the board edges, to smooth down materials, to burnish board, and for about a hundred other uses. The essential bookbinder's tool, the bone folder, is a flat, smooth tool carved from bone in a variety of shapes and sizes. The most useful is a 6"–8" (15–20 cm) folder, with one pointed and

one rounded end. Teflon folders are generally thicker than bone folders and cannot fit into the narrow spaces where bone folders can slide. Their advantage over the bone tool is in smoothing down glued materials; miraculously, they do not mark or score the surface of cloth when rubbed directly on top of a cloth-covered board.

KNIVES: Utility or mat knives, X-acto knives or knives with snap-off blades are all acceptable and easily available at hardware and art supply stores. For most operations I prefer a surgical scalpel (#4 handle) and good-quality curved blades (#23), purchased through bookbinding or surgical suppliers. For cutting binder's board, a utility knife is best.

MICRO-SPATULA: A slender, metal surgical tool with flattened ends, used to push ribbons through narrow slits; from bookbinding and surgical suppliers.

POTTER'S NEEDLE: A sewing needle stuck into a metal or wooden handle. Finer than an awl, it is useful for making unobtrusive pinpricks on materials prior to punching or chiseling; from a pottery supplier.

PRESSING BOARDS: All of the projects in this book require gentle pressing—that is, under boards and weights rather than in a bookbinding press. Plywood, hardwood, and seasoned masonite boards, sheets of heavy-duty plastic, and leftover kitchen counter laminates in all sizes are useful. Boards must be larger than the item being pressed.

RULERS: A metal ruler or straight-edge is preferable to a plastic

one that can be nicked or shaved when used with a knife. The heavier the ruler, the more secure the action.

SANDPAPER: Used to smooth the seams of a box after gluing-up. To make your own sanding sticks, glue various grades of sandpaper to heavyweight binder's board; cut the boards into $1^{1}/_{2}$"–2" (4–5 cm) wide strips, 10"–12" (25-30 cm) in length.

SCISSORS: Make sure they're good and sharp. Used mostly for rough cutting of cloth, trimming corners, snipping ribbons, etc. Most accurate cutting is done with a knife and straight-edge or, for the truly fortunate, with a heavy-duty board shears.

SEWING NEEDLES: A variety of needles, with large and small eyes, is useful.

SPRING DIVIDER: A measuring device (similar to a compass in appearance) used to obtain measurements and transfer them to subsequent steps in the boxmaking process. This wonderful tool limits dependence on numbers (and on math in general). Next to the bone folder, it is the bookbinder's best friend; from bookbinding and architectural tool suppliers.

T-SQUARE: Used, with a knife, for cutting boards (and other materials) and maintaining right angles; from an art supply store.

TRIANGLE: You can't make boxes without a metal triangle. The smaller the better, to fit into the right-angled corners of little boxes; from a bookbinding or art supply store.

WEIGHTS: Anything will work: bricks wrapped in bookcloth to keep them clean, tins filled with pennies or with sand, small dressmaking weights, or hefty litho stones.

OTHER IMPORTANT SUPPLIES INCLUDE THE FOLLOWING:

- Waste paper: Vital in all steps of boxmaking, to keep both workbench and box surfaces free of adhesives. Must be thin and absorbent. The best paper is unprinted newsprint, available in pads from art supply stores or in bundles from packing and moving businesses.
- Pencils and pencil sharpener.
- Bowls, for glue and paste.
- Measuring cup and spoons, for preparing adhesives.
- Whisk and pot, for cooking paste.
- Paper towels.
- Plastic containers with lids, to store adhesives.
- Wax paper.
- Masking tape.
- Hammer or mallet, for use with chisels and punches.
- Trash can.

the essentials: *materials*

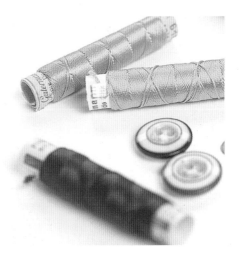

The basic materials of boxmaking are paper, cloth, board, and adhesives.

PAPER

The world of papers is large and magnificent. Art supply and stationery stores, Asian groceries, a trunk in the attic or at the flea market, today's mail—all are potential sources for treasures. Whether cheap and gaudy or handmade and elegant, nothing transforms a box from ordinary to extraordinary more swiftly than the right piece of paper.

Papers vary greatly in strength and durability and must be used appropriately. Papers too fragile to function as hinges work beautifully as box liners. Papers too thick to mold themselves around boards are simply scored and left to stand as paper boxes. Papers too sheer to hide the construction details of the box are either laminated or carded around lightweight boards to make them denser. All papers have a place in boxmaking.

CLOTH

The world of bookcloth is smaller than that of paper. Bookcloth is fabric that has been treated to accept the application of adhesives.

Most commonly, fabrics are backed with paper to provide a glue barrier. Older cloths, such as starch-filled muslins and lovely glazed buckrams, are slowly disappearing. Paper-backed rayon, silk, and linen, in dazzling colors and various textures, are taking over the market.

Cloth must be used wherever there is extensive hinging. In combination with decorative papers, cloth is often used in narrow strips to cover the joints of the box. To learn how to convert your own fabric into bookcloth, see The Picture Frame Box, page 41.

BOARD

Binder's board is an extremely dense cardboard and is available in an acid-free form. I use three thicknesses—60 point (lightweight), 80 point (medium weight), and 100 point (heavyweight) board.

Rag boards, such as museum and mat boards, are easier to cut than binder's board but are also easier to dent. Because of their high cotton content, rag boards are thirsty, slurping up the moisture from adhesives and thus are more likely to warp than binder's board.

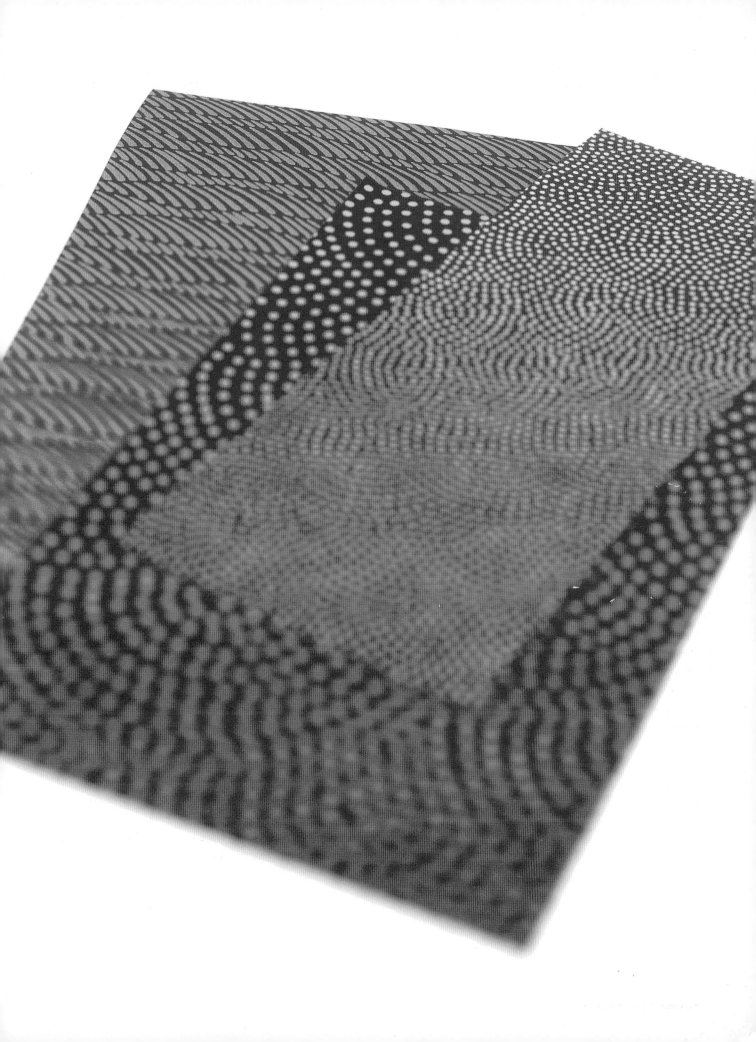

the essentials: *adhesives*

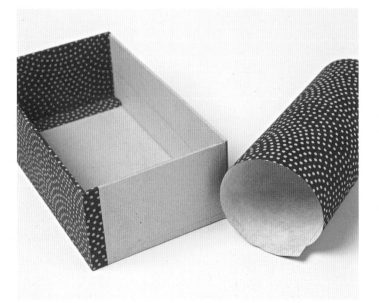

ADHESIVES

Most bookbinders have a love/hate relationship with adhesives: We need them, but they cause much heartache. The rules governing their use.change according to the project. No two boxes, by either their materials or their size, ever seem alike. And the rules of adhesives are based completely on: (1) the properties of the materials (paper-covered boxes require an entirely different approach than cloth-covered boxes), and (2) the size of the box (large boxes have a different set of rules than small boxes). To tell you that experience must be your guide in the selection of the proper adhesive seems evasive. It is, however, the truest piece of advice I can give. I use four adhesives: Paste, glue, methyl cellulose, and assorted pressure-sensitive adhesives.

WHY ADHESIVES MATTER

Buckling and warping in boxes are due to either a miscalculation in grain direction or to the improper use of an adhesive coupled with inadequate drying techniques.

Most adhesives contain moisture. Moisture causes materials to stretch and expand. Materials that expand eventually try to contract. This contraction causes warping. Because warping cannot be avoided, it must be counteracted.

Try this experiment: Cut two pieces of paper and one piece of binder's board, all to the same dimensions and grain direction

(see page 14). Paste out one piece of paper. Notice how the paper has stretched in width (from spine to fore edge). Apply the pasted paper to the board. Observe the board. Within minutes, the board will begin to curve, first away from and then toward the paper-covered surface. At this point, all the pressure in the world will not flatten the board. Paste out the second piece of paper and apply it to the reverse side of the board.

Observe the board. Initially, the original warp will increase until, slowly, the board pulls back in the opposite direction and eventually flattens. At this point, pressing the board under a light weight will help stabilize it.

The lesson is this: Whatever you do to one side of a board, do to the other. Keep the moisture content consistent. In order to be consistent you must sometimes fool your materials. For example, if you are covering a box with cloth (using mixture) but lining it with a delicate paper (requiring paste), add an extra dollop of methyl cellulose to your mixture—make it wetter and thereby induce more warp, to counteract the reverse warp of the pasted surface.

PASTE

Paste, vegetable in origin, is a flour or a starch cooked with water. Rice starch, wheat starch, and the unbleached flour in your kitchen pantry all make fine pastes.

I use paste exclusively on paper—never on cloth or boards. Paste is the most luscious adhesive: Smooth and creamy in the bowl, it spreads like silk across the surface of a sheet of paper. Largely water in content, paste induces the immediate relaxation of even the crankiest papers. Fragile papers that tear under the weight of glue and stubborn papers (like gift wrap) that escape into sticky spirals unless they are thoroughly subdued with water are the best candidates for paste.

ADVANTAGES OF PASTE

- Paste is reversible with water. Stains can sometimes be removed with a damp sponge.
- Paste dries slowly. If you need the adhesive to stay active for a long time (as when covering a large box), use paste. If the paste is drying more quickly than expected, it can be reset by spritzing the pasted paper with water.

DISADVANTAGES OF PASTE

- Paste requires cooking. (There are some precooked flour pastes on the market, but they are somewhat gritty.)
- Paste has a short life once cooked.
  Since most preservatives are either toxic (thymol) or aggressively scented (oil of cloves, oil of wintergreen), I prefer to make small batches of paste daily rather than to use preservatives. Refrigeration prolongs the life of a bowl of paste, but it also makes the paste watery and less sticky.

INGREDIENTS Yield: Approximately 1 cup of paste.
- 4 tablespoons rice starch
- 1/4 cup cold water
- 1/2 to 1 cup boiling water
- (Note that these amounts are approximate. Can be thinned by adding cold water.)

Measure the starch into a saucepan. Add the cold water and whisk until the starch is completely dissolved. Add 1/2 cup of the boiling water, slowly, as you continue to whisk. Place the saucepan over a medium flame and cook, stirring constantly and adding more water as necessary, until the mixture thickens and turns translucent. When the mixture comes to a boil, let it cook for a minute or so. Remove the saucepan from the stove and pour the paste into a bowl to cool. Stir occasionally to prevent a skin from forming.

GLUE

There are many glues, both animal in origin (hide, rabbit skin, fish) and synthetic. In boxmaking I use one of the synthetic glues, polyvinyl acetate (PVA). There are several PVAs on the market; select an acid-free one. Because it is extremely tacky and unspreadable, I rarely use full-strength PVA. For maximum bond in dealing with small details (as in tipping a ribbon tie into position), I dip directly into my jar of glue. But for most operations I dilute the PVA with methyl cellulose (see page 12). Methyl cellulose makes the PVA easier to spread and slows its drying time. This combination of PVA/methyl cellulose will be referred to as mixture throughout these pages.

ADVANTAGES OF GLUE

- PVA requires no preparation.
- PVA has a long shelf life. (It must, however, be protected from freezing.)
- PVA dries quickly.

DISADVANTAGES OF GLUE

- Most PVAs are not reversible with water. It is almost impossible to remove glue stains from cloth and paper.
- PVA dries quickly. If working time is required, the PVA must be diluted.

METHYL CELLULOSE

Methyl cellulose is a synthetic adhesive. Because it does not have especially strong bonding qualities, I do not use methyl cellulose as an independent adhesive. Its use in boxmaking is as an additive to PVA. This resulting mixture is used on all cloth work, on most board operations, and on many heavy-weight papers.

In the mixture you will use, the proportion of the methyl cellulose to the PVA will vary according to the strength of the prepared methyl cellulose (it comes in granular form and must be mixed with water) and the scale of the work involved. If more time is needed (as in covering a large box), add an extra dollop of methyl cellulose to your bowl of mixture.

ADVANTAGES OF METHYL CELLULOSE

- Once prepared, methyl cellulose can be stored in a sealed container for weeks.
- It is reversible with water.
- It makes PVA a workable adhesive.

DISADVANTAGES OF METHYL CELLULOSE

- It has limited bonding qualities.
- It requires (minimal) preparation.

INGREDIENTS

2 teaspoons methyl cellulose

1 cup cold water

(Note that these amounts are approximate).

Pour the cup of cold water into a container. Sprinkle methyl cellulose into the water. Whisk vigorously. Let stand several hours until solution becomes uniformly gel-like and translucent. Store in a lidded container. Shake well before using.

PRESSURE-SENSITIVE ADHESIVES

Pressure-sensitive adhesives are layers of adhesives backed on release papers. I depend on these adhesives when moisture must be kept entirely out of a project, for example, when mounting a photograph on a box cover. They are also convenient in assembling scored boxes.

ADVANTAGES OF PRESSURE-SENSITIVE ADHESIVES

- They are moisture free.
- Their bond is immediate—no pressing or drying time is required.

DISADVANTAGES OF PRESSURE-SENSITIVE ADHESIVES

- The bond is immediate, allowing no slip time to guide the materials into position.
- Many of them are not archival. Consult your supplier's catalog for specifics.

the basics

This is the most important chapter in the book. All of my projects refer to the techniques and processes described here. There is a comforting repetitive quality to the steps involved in boxmaking. In the beginning you will refer to these pages often. Soon, you will not even need to peek at them.

THE PARTS OF THE BOX

A box is composed of several separate units: The case, the flaps, the tray, and the lid. The case, consisting of a front, spine, and back, is constructed by assembling the boards on the covering material, often leaving a space between the boards (called a *joint*) to act as a hinge.

The most basic box is a simple case with no flaps, no trays, and no lid.

Flaps are panels attached to the case at the top (head), bottom (tail), and side (fore edge). They can be made separately and glued onto the case (as in The Artist's Portfolio), or they can grow from the case itself (The Postcard Box). Flaps keep the contents of the box from falling out.

Trays consist of base boards with walls glued to them prior to covering. Trays are three-walled or four-walled, depending on the style of box.

Lids, either freestanding or attached to the spine, are panels built to extend slightly beyond the parameters of a tray. They create a lip for easy accessibility and lifting and are often embellished with knobs, buttons, ribbons, and other fasteners.

GRAIN DIRECTION

Anyone who has ever torn an article out of a newspaper has had a lesson in grain direction: Pulled in one direction, the paper tears beautifully. But when pulled in the perpendicular direction, the paper rips jaggedly. The clean tear is with the grain; the ragged one, against the grain.

Grain is inherent in paper, cloth, and board. It is determined by an alignment of fibers. The direction in which most of the fibers are aligned is the grain direction of the material.

WHY GRAIN MATTERS

For the moveable parts of a box to work easily and without stress, the grain must run parallel to this hinging action. In a book, grain runs parallel to its spine, making it easy to turn the pages and manipulate the cover. The same is true in boxmaking. The grain must run parallel to the spine of the box.

Understanding grain direction is also important for predicting the stretch of materials as they come in contact with moisture (adhesives). Materials expand *opposite* their grain direction. If a piece of lining paper is cut to fit perfectly within a box, after pasting it will have stretched in width (against its grain) while having remained unchanged in height (with the grain). It is necessary to anticipate this stretch and to trim paper accordingly before pasting or gluing.

HOW TO DETERMINE GRAIN

The best way to determine grain is through your sense of touch.

For paper and cloth, gently bend (don't crease!) the material and roll it back and forth several times. Let the paper or cloth relax, then bend and roll it in the opposite direction. The direction in which you feel the least resistance is the grain direction.

For board, hold a corner in both hands and flex it, then release the board. Flex the board in the opposite direction. The flexing direction of least resistance is the grain direction.

the basics: *measuring and cutting*

CUTTING

In addition to the hand tools described earlier, a wonderful piece of equipment is a paper cutter. Whether tabletop or freestanding, a paper cutter (or the more substantial *board shears*) makes the difference between easy and laborious cutting. A good cutter that has a bed with a true edge perpendicular to the cutting edge, a clamp to hold the material in place, and a pair of sharp upper and lower knives is a joy to use. If a cutter is not available, use a utility knife and a T-square.

To ensure accuracy in cutting, you must follow a four-step process.

1. Determine grain direction of the board. (Review Grain Direction on page 14 if you need help with this.) Grain direction must run from head to tail on all boards.

2. Rough cut the board to the approximate size needed for the box. An oversized board is difficult to handle and will not fit on a tabletop paper cutter.

3. Square the board by trimming one long edge of board and a perpendicular short edge to form a true right angle.

4. Mark the board by placing the object to be boxed on the squared corner and making penciled markings of desired height and width.

To determine the depth of the object to be boxed, crease a scrap of paper to form a right angle; slide this scrap under the object and make a parallel crease in the scrap paper, snugly enclosing the object within these two creases. Transfer this measurement—the distance from one crease to the other—to your board.

MEASURING

All boxes start from the inside out. The first piece of board to be measured and cut is the base board, the piece on which your objects (books, photos, marbles) will sit. All of the other boards take their measurements from the base. The base has two dimensions: Height and width.

Height is the distance from top to bottom or, in the bookbinder's language (used throughout this book), from *head* to *tail*. *Width* is the distance from side to side or, more precisely, from *spine* to *fore-edge*. The third dimension of the box, its *depth*, is found in its walls. Depth refers to the thickness of the object to be boxed; the distance, for example, from the top card to the bottom card in a deck of cards.

My approach to measuring is more intuitive than mathematical; I rarely rely on numbers. I love my rulers for their straight edges, not for their numbered markings. Precision is achieved by paying attention to the relationships between the materials and the parts of the box. This book provides you with models to be altered for future projects. When you understand the relationships between the parts and the whole, you will be able to change my patterns and create entirely new boxes.

the basics: *pasting and gluing*

PASTING AND GLUING

Pasting refers to the use of any starch-based adhesive. Gluing refers to the use of both full-strength PVA and the more commonly applied mixture of PVA and methyl cellulose.

PAPER   Some papers demand paste; others are happier with the PVA/methyl cellulose mixture. In general, lightweight papers that tend to stretch and curl excessively prefer paste. The high water content in paste saturates the paper and makes it lie down and behave. Similarly, thin, long-fibered translucent papers—like many Japanese tissues—respond better to paste than to mixture. Use mixture on heavyweight papers, which are unlikely to curl and stretch.

CLOTH AND BOARDS   On cloth and boards, always use the PVA/methyl cellulose mixture. The only question is how much PVA? How much methyl cellulose? The answer is determined by the size of your box, the nature of your materials, and the consistency of both adhesives. Remember, a larger box requires more working time (i.e., more moisture) than a smaller box. I usually start with a combination of approximately 70% PVA and 30% methyl cellulose. If my brush drags rather than glides across the surface being glued, my adhesive is too dry. I stop brushing and add another dollop of methyl cellulose to the mixture.

HOW TO PASTE A SHEET OF PAPER TO BOARD

When covering a board with paper, the adhesive must be applied to the paper rather than to the board. If dry paper is pressed onto a wet board, the paper will wrinkle. To paste, place a few layers of newsprint on the workbench. The newsprint should be larger than the paper being pasted. Position your paper face down on the newsprint. Scoop up a generous amount of paste with your paste brush and apply it to the paper with a circular motion, starting at the center of the piece of paper and working outward in concentric circles. Be sure one hand anchors the paper firmly to the newsprint. Keep a paper towel nearby, as you will get paste on your fingers. As you approach the edges of the paper, stop making circles. Return to the center of the paper and brush outward, in radiating strokes, creating a sunburst pattern. Never hold the brush parallel with the edges of the paper: Bristles can slip underneath and stain the surface of the paper. Give the pasted sheet of paper plenty of time to relax before picking it up. If the paper is curling excessively, continue to work your brush across the surface, pressing and flattening. When the paper has been sufficiently saturated with moisture, it will lie flat. Pick up the paper and apply it to the board.

HOW TO GLUE CLOTH TO BOARD

Unlike adhering paper to board, the adhesive can be applied to either the board or the cloth. To glue, follow all procedures as described above, substituting your glue brush for the paste brush and adjusting the PVA/methyl cellulose mixture to suit your materials.

HOW TO CONSTRUCT THE TRAY   C-clamp a wooden board onto your tabletop. Set down a piece of wax paper. Place the base board on the wax paper. Using full-strength PVA and a small brush, paint a thin line of glue along the edge of the head wall where it touches the base. Position this wall against the clamped wooden board and push the base against it. (The clamped board supports the wall and helps to maintain a right angle.) Wipe away excess glue with your bone folder. Glue the fore-edge wall, painting the glue along the edge touching the base and also along the edge that meets the head wall. Glue the tail wall, painting the glue along the edge touching the base and also along the edge that meets the fore-edge wall. Glue the spine wall, painting the glue along the edge touching the base and also along the two edges that meet the head and tail walls. Let the tray set until it is dry (15 minutes). Peel the tray off the wax paper, and sand any rough joints. The tray is now ready for covering.

HOW TO COVER THE TRAY WITH PAPER

COVERING THE OUTSIDE   Cut a piece of paper long enough to wrap around all walls, plus ¹/₂" (1 cm). (If your decorative paper is not long enough, use two shorter pieces; plan the seam to fall at a corner.) In width, the paper should be twice the depth of the tray, plus 1 ¹/₂" (4 cm).

Paste out the paper. Give the paper time to relax and uncurl. Position your tray, with the bottom of the tray facing you, approximately ³/₄" (2 cm) away from the long edge of the paper and ¹/₂" (1 cm) away from the short edge. Crease the ¹/₂" (1 cm) extension around the corner and onto the wall.

Roll the tray on the paper, pushing the tray snugly into each right angle as it is formed. Before making the final roll, check the paper for stretch. If the paper has stretched beyond the board edge, trim

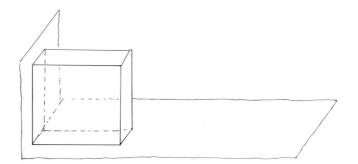

it to fit. Remember, wet paper tends to tear. To minimize this risk, place a piece of wax paper on top of the paper to be trimmed, and cut through the wax paper, using a sawing motion with your knife. Use your bone folder to crease the ³/₄" (2 cm) turn-ins onto the bottom of the tray. Clip the corners with scissors, and press the paper into position. You are now ready to finish the inside of the tray.

FINISHING THE INSIDE   (above left) To finish the inside of the tray, slivers of paper exactly one board thickness in width must be removed at each of the four corners. Position the tray on its spine wall, on a cutting mat. Place your metal triangle on the paper. One edge of the triangle should touch the board edge (thickness) while the triangle is slid firmly into the curve of the wrapped paper in the left-hand corner. With your knife, cut through the paper. Start the cut with the tip of the knife actually touching the board. Make a parallel cut, one board thickness away from the original cut. **Important:** Do not start this cut at the board. With the triangle repositioned, place the knife 1 ¹/₂ board thicknesses away from the board, and cut. With your knife, make a diagonal cut between the starting points of these two parallel cuts. This cut releases the sliver of paper—one board thickness in width—which allows the covering paper to be turned neatly into the inside of the tray. It also creates a mitered corner. Keeping the tray resting on its spine wall, repeat these cuts in the right-hand corner.

Turn the tray onto its fore-edge wall. Make the cuts, as described previously, in first the left and then the right-hand corners. **Note:** These cuts are made in only two of the tray's four walls. I have selected the opposite spine and fore-edge walls; you could pick the other pair of opposites, the head and tail walls. Your final cuts are made with scissors. Push the spine wall covering into the tray, pressing it against the inside wall and forcing the paper into the right-angle where the base meets the spine wall. Gently crease the paper by running your bone folder along this seam. Pull the paper back to the outside and cut away the two corners, removing 45-degree triangles of paper. Make sure the cuts stop at the crease mark made in the previous step. Repeat with the fore-edge wall.

(above middle) You are now ready to paste. Starting with the head, paste out the covering paper and push it to the inside, pressing it sharply into all seams. Rub with your bone folder to eliminate air bubbles and paste lumps. Repeat at the tail. (Since these two wall coverings have not had slivers of paper removed from them, they overlap the corners. This ensures that the cardboard seam will be covered.) Paste out the spine wall covering and press into place. Paste out the fore edge wall covering and press into place (above right).

the basics: *corners and finishing edges*

HOW TO COVER THE TRAY WITH CLOTH

When covering a small tray in cloth, I follow the same procedure described above, substituting mixture for paste.

When covering a large tray in cloth, I prefer to glue out the boards—one wall at a time—rather than the cloth, and to work a bit more slowly. Take care to press down the fabric well as you roll the tray on the cloth. Wrinkles in the cloth are more likely to develop if the cloth has not been saturated with the adhesive.

COVERING BOARDS: CUTTING CORNERS AND FINISHING EDGES

Cover papers and cloths are cut to extend $^3/_4$" (2 cm) beyond the edges of the board to be covered. This extension is called the "turn-in." Before the covering material is turned in, its corners must be cut. Both the angle of the cut and its distance from the tip of the board are crucial.

Apply adhesive to the covering material and press the board into position. Trim the corners at a 45-degree angle. The distance between the tip of the board and this cut should measure $1^1/_2$ times the thickness of the board. If you cut too closely, the tip of the board is exposed. If you cut too far away, the corner is klutzy. After cutting all corners, re-apply adhesive to the turn-ins if necessary.

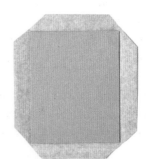

Starting with the head and tail, bring the turn-ins onto the board. First, using your bone folder, crease the material against the board edge. Second, flatten the material onto the board, pressing out any air pockets or bubbles. Use your thumbnail to pinch in the small sharp triangles of material at the corners. Press firmly so that the material hugs the corner and molds itself around the board tip. Now bring the spine and fore-edge turn-ins onto the board. With your folder, gently tap all corners, eliminating any sharp points or loose threads.

ALTERNATE CORNER COVERING FOR FRAGILE PAPERS

When wet, fragile or thin papers tend to tear. A universal or library corner involves no cutting and is recommended. This treatment is inappropriate for heavyweight papers or cloth; the resulting corner would be too bulky. After pasting the paper and centering the board on it, fold one corner triangle onto the board. Using your bone folder, shape the paper against the board thickness on both top (head) and side (fore-edge). Firmly press the remaining bits (right side of paper) onto the turn-ins below. Repeat at the other corners. With your finger, dab a dot of paste onto the turn-ins, near the corners. Complete the turn-ins (as in above directions). This corner covering yields a gentle, slightly rounded corner.

I hoard travel postcards of places seen and unseen. Quite apart from the memories or the dreams they evoke, picture postcards are cheap miniature works of art. At flea markets, great treasures abound for a buck! The beauty of The Postcard Box is the simplicity of its construction: All of the boards are cut out in advance, then glued to a single piece of cloth. There is also a wonderful economy of time and materials. Many of the boards share the same dimensions and are cut with a minimum of measuring. And the scrap fabric is recycled in the finishing. My box is built to hold a 2" (5 cm) stack of postcards.

postcard box...
memories of travels both real and imagined

MATERIALS

Binder's board, 60 point	1 button (or more, for decorating)	PVA, mixture and paste
Bookcloth		Pressure-sensitive adhesive
Decorative paper	1 postcard or photograph	
Elastic cord	Sewing thread	

getting started:
gathering the decorations

- Gather the contents of the box: postcards received from friends and family, postcards from your travels or handmade postcards.
- Collect buttons: One will serve as the clasp, so make sure it is sturdy. The others will be for decoration.
- Decide on decorative paper to line the inside of the box.

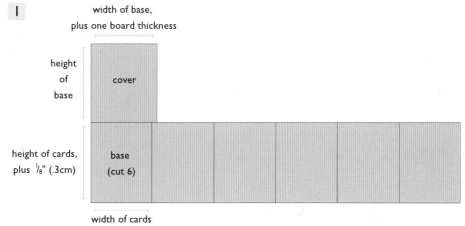

| 1 | width of base, plus one board thickness |

height of base — cover

height of cards, plus $1/8$" (.3cm) — base (cut 6)

width of cards plus $1/8$" (.3cm)

CUT OUT ALL OF THE BOARDS

Cut out all of the boards, following the layout above. Cut 6 pieces to:

Height = height of postcards plus $1/8$" (.3 cm)
Width = width of postcards plus $1/8$" (.3 cm)

Remember: grain must run from head to tail. Label one piece "base," and set it aside. Label one piece "fore-edge flap," and set it aside. Cut one piece in half, crosswise; trim a sliver off each piece, crosswise. Label these boards "head flap" and "tail flap," and set them aside.

Cut two 2" (5 cm) deep strips off one of the remaining boards, crosswise. Label these boards "head wall" and "tail wall." Cut a lengthwise strip, 2" (5 cm) plus one board thickness in width, from one of the remaining boards. Label it "fore-edge

wall." From the last remaining board cut a lengthwise strip that measures 2" (5 cm) plus two board thicknesses in width. Label it "spine wall." If you wish to make a shallower or deeper box, adjust the depth of these walls accordingly. You have now used up all six pieces. The final board, the cover board, is cut separately. Cut a board to:
Height = height of base board
Width = width of base board plus one board thickness
Label this piece "cover." From a leftover board, cut a narrow strip a scant two board-thicknesses in width (grain long for ease in cutting). This will be your joint spacer. You need only one spacer; it will be re-used several times.

2 CUT A PIECE OF BOOKCLOTH large enough to accommodate all of the boards with a generous margin. This box requires a piece of cloth approximately 22" (56 cm) square. Trim off the selvage, or bound edge, of the cloth. Do not trim any other cloth until the boards have been glued into place.

GLUE THE BOARDS ONTO THE CLOTH. Place the cloth, wrong side up, on newsprint. Arrange the boards on the cloth, making sure the grain direction of the cloth and the board is the same. On a separate stack of newsprint, glue the boards one at a time and press them onto the cloth. The same spacer will be used between all of the boards (see drawing). Start with the cover board and work your way across the horizontal plane before gluing the vertical elements. When all of the boards are in place, turn the cloth over and rub down with your folder to make sure no air bubbles remain.

TRIM THE TURN-IN MARGINS. Cut a scrap board to approximately ³/₄" (2 cm). Use it to trace around the edges of the boards, drawing the turn-in allowance. Slide a cutting mat under the cloth and trim, using a knife and straight-edge.

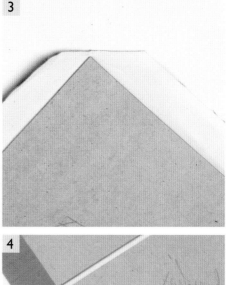

3 CUT THE CLOTH at the four corners of the base board, slicing diagonally through the turn-in, cutting in as close as possible to the tip of the board. Cut off the (8) triangles at the outer corners of the boards. (See The Basics, page 22.) Stay 1¹/₂ board thicknesses away from the tip of the boards.

4 GLUE THE TURN-INS. Start with the eight turn-ins that touch the walls; finish with the four turn-ins that land on the flaps. Use your ¹/₂" (1 cm) brush. Before gluing, slip narrow strips of newsprint under each turn-in. Glue. Remove the waste strip and press the cloth against the board edge. With the edge of your bone folder, work the cloth into the two joints, pressing back and forth until the fabric has stuck. With the broad side of your bone folder, press the cloth onto the boards. Work through a waste sheet to prevent marking the cloth.

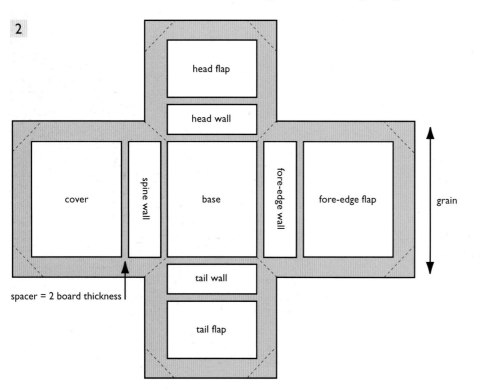

2

head flap

head wall

cover

spine wall

base

fore-edge wall

fore-edge flap

grain

tail wall

tail flap

spacer = 2 board thickness

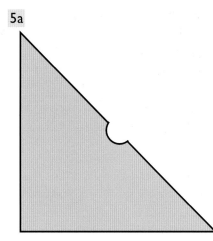

5a COVER THE TIPS OF THE BASE BOARD. Cut four triangles from the fabric off-cuts and trim them to fit the corners of the base board. They should match up with, and complete, the edges of the turn-ins. Do not overlap the fabric. If necessary, scoop out a slight crescent shape along the long side of the triangle to keep the right angle formed by the vertical and horizontal planes clean and crisp.

5b Glue out one triangle. Press it lightly onto the base board. Immediately work the fabric into the two joints, pressing back and forth with your bone folder.

5c Mold the cloth around the tip of the board, patting down any loose threads. Repeat with the other three triangles.

tip Allow a ³/₄" (2 cm) margin of cloth around all board edges. Reserve the left-over bits of fabric for finishing details. This box requires a piece of cloth approximately 22" (56 cm) square.

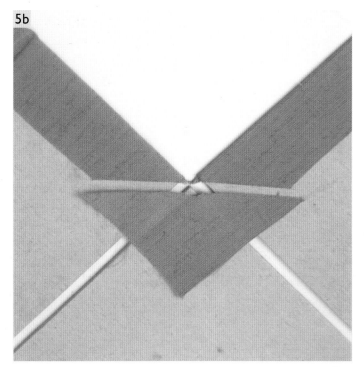

6a

6a DECORATE THE BOX. This is the box's best moment: When you choose a card and a handful of buttons and make your box an object of delight. Design the cover. Include in your design one button that will be the box's closure. If affixing a photograph or a postcard, use a pressure-sensitive adhesive to adhere the artwork to the cover; eventually, the card will be sewn into place. Arrange the button(s) on the cover. Punch holes through the boards to correspond with the button holes. Sew on the button(s).

6b

6b Note: If not incorporating buttons into your design, punch holes through the card in strategic places—the corners, for example—and stitch the card in place. The pressure-sensitive adhesive is not secure enough for permanent attachment. Punch two holes in the fore-edge wall for the elastic cord. Thread both ends of the cord through the holes; adjust cord for the proper tension. If desired, thread a button or two onto the cord, to disguise these holes. Cut two shallow channels in the board and tip down the ends of the cord using undiluted PVA. Be persistent: The elastic does not want to stick! Press with your folder to flatten the cord. One or two careful hits with a hammer sometimes does the trick.

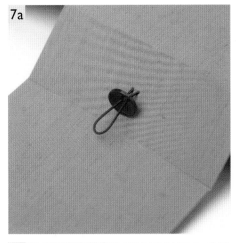

7a

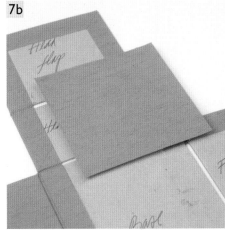

7b

8

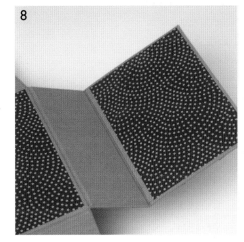

7a **COVER THE INSIDE WALLS.**
Cut four strips of cloth from your leftovers.
These strips will extend from the base
board to the flaps, covering the walls. They
are cut to fit approximately one board
thickness away from the outer edges of
the box. Cut two strips for the spine and
fore-edge walls:
Height = height of walls minus two board
thicknesses
Width = depth of walls plus 2" (5 cm)
Cut two strips for the head and tail walls:
Height = depth of wall plus 2" (5 cm)
Width = width of walls minus two board
thicknesses

7b Grain should run from head to tail.
Glue out the spine wall covering. Position
the cloth on the base board, even with the
turn-ins and centered heightwise. With the
edge of your bone folder, quickly press the
cloth into the joint nearest the base; smooth
the cloth across the spine wall; press it into
the second joint; smooth the cloth onto
the cover board. Repeat with the other three
wall coverings.

8 **LINE THE BOX.** Cut five pieces of
paper to line all panels of the box. These
papers are cut to fit approximately one
board thickness away from all four edges

VARIATION

VARIATION

This box is a fine container for photographs as well as postcards. To protect
the fragile edges of vintage materials,
such as this nineteenth-century portrait,
frame the artwork prior to sewing it
onto the cover. In keeping with the
spirit of the photograph, I have used
a piece of a handwritten document
(also nineteenth century and found
in a flea market) to protect and to
celebrate this photographic gem.

ROBERT WARNER
Emily Dickinson Box

This box, with its mix of color and pattern, is a quilt-maker's dream. Just reach into your scrap bag, and use whatever bits and pieces come to hand. The box follows the same architectural layout as The Postcard Box but is made in three independent units assembled to form a whole. Because it is built of separate pieces, the design possibilities are vast. I've made my box as exuberant as possible by using different colored cloths to cover the walls and an assortment of decorative papers inside and out. The angling of the head and tail flaps can take many shapes. The cover and the fore-edge panels can be similarly altered.

the patchwork box...
memories of Grandmother's quilts

MATERIALS

Binder's board

Assorted odds and end of Bookcloth

Assorted odds and ends of decorative papers

Ribbon

PVA, mixture and paste

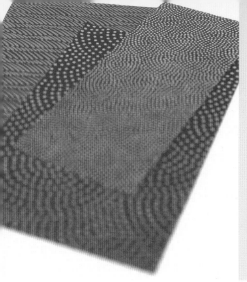

getting started:
gathering materials

• Collect the letters and other memorabilia for the box.
• Make sure your collected materials will fit in the box.

1   **CUT THE BOARDS.** Follow the same cutting layout as in The Postcard Box (page 25). Angle the head and tail flaps, as desired.

CUT THE CLOTH. Cloth must be used to cover the walls and the joints of the box where hinging occurs. The amount of cloth that extends beyond the joints is entirely up to you. The measurements below provide for $^1/_2$" (1 cm) coverage. Vary them to suit your own sense of design.

Cut two pieces of cloth to cover the spine and fore-edge walls:
Height = height of boards plus $1^1/_2$" (4 cm)
Width = depth of wall plus $1^3/_4$" (4.5 cm)

Cut two pieces of cloth to cover the head and tail walls:
Height = depth of wall plus 2" (5 cm)
Width = width of boards plus $1^1/_2$" (4 cm)

1

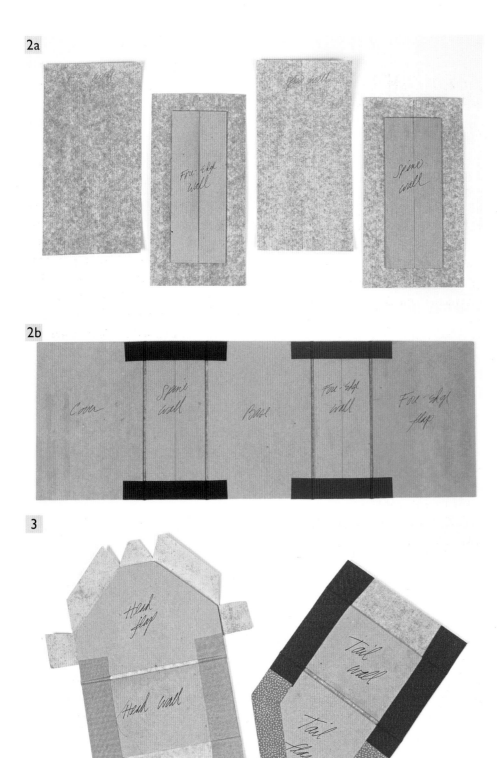

2a   CONSTRUCT THE CASE. Locate the center of the spine and fore-edge walls and draw a light pencil line from top to bottom. Repeat with spine and fore-edge cloth. Glue out (with mixture) the spine wall; center the board on the cloth; press. Do not glue the turn-ins. Glue out (with mixture) the fore-edge wall; center the board on the cloth; press. Do not glue the turn-ins.

2b   Place the spine wall on a stack of waste papers, larger than the cloth strips by a couple of inches. Glue out the cloth to the left of the wall; remove the waste sheet. Rest the joint spacer against the left-hand side of the wall and push the cover board against the spacer, aligning the height of the boards. Press quickly and pluck out the spacer. Repeat these steps on the right-hand side of the spine wall to attach the base board.

Place the fore-edge wall on the stack of waste sheets. Glue out the cloth to the left of the wall, insert the joint spacer, and push the base board firmly against the spacer. Repeat on right hand side to attach the fore-edge flap.

Glue out the turn-ins and bring the cloth onto the boards, pushing the fabric firmly into the joints of the case.

3   CONSTRUCT THE HEAD AND TAIL UNITS. These two units need more generously measured strips of cloth than the spine and fore-edge walls. A 1" (3 cm) extension of cloth will become the hinge attaching the head and tail flaps to the case. Glue out the head wall and position it approximately ³/₄" (2 cm) away from one long edge of cloth, centered left to right. Working on a stack of waste sheets, glue out the ³/₄" (2 cm) extension; remove the upper waste sheet. Gently rest the joint spacer against the wall and push the head flap firmly against the spacer. Press quickly and pluck out the spacer. Repeat with the tail wall and tail flap. Glue out the two short turn-ins on each unit. With the edge of your bone folder, work the cloth crisply into the joint. Pat into place on the boards. Make sure that the turn-ins and the 1" (3 cm) (hinge) extension have been thoroughly pressed together.

4

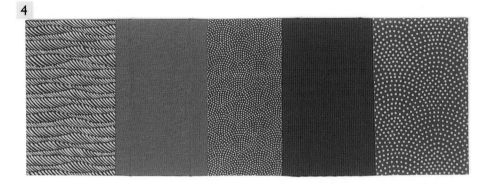

4 CUT AND APPLY THE DECORATIVE PAPERS (case). Cut two pieces of paper for the cover and fore-edge flaps:
Height = height of boards plus 1 ¹/₂" (4 cm)
Width = distance from edge of cloth to edge of board plus ³/₄" (2 cm)
Cut one piece of paper for the base board:
Height = height of boards plus 1 ¹/₂" (4 cm)
Width = distance between both cloth edges plus ¹/₄" (.5 cm)
Note: These papers will be pasted slightly (¹/₁₆"–¹/₈" [.15cm–.3 cm]) over the edge of the cloth to prevent the cloth from unraveling and to insure uniform and total coverage of the board. To accurately position your paper, mark both cover and fore-edge flap. Set your spring divider to a measure just short of the distance between the edge of the wall board and the edge of the cloth; pierce the cloth, near the head and tail. Repeat this procedure on the base board, marking only one of the two fabric edges.

Prepare waste sheets. Paste out the cover paper and position it on the case, covering the two guide marks. Make sure the paper is centered. Working through a waste sheet, press first with your hands and then with your folder. Take care not to press too vigorously along the edge overlapping the cloth; paste could seep out and stain the fabric. Flip the case over, cut the corners and finish the edges. (See The Basics, page 22). Repeat with the fore-edge paper.
Note: Do not cut corners off the base paper. Simply bring the turn-ins onto the board and press with your folder. Sandwich case between dry waste sheets, place under a board and a weight, and put it aside.

5 CUT AND APPLY DECORATIVE PAPERS (head and tail flaps). Cut two pieces of paper:
Height = distance from edge of cloth to board edge plus ³/₄" (2 cm)
Width = width of boards plus 1 ¹/₂" (3 cm)
Pierce guide marks on cloth; paste out paper; apply paper to board and press (as in Step 6). Fold and unfold the turn-ins a few times, see where there is too much bulk, cut out a few V-shaped pieces—staying, always one board thickness away from the board edge. Re-apply paste to the turn-ins and press them onto the board. Put aside, under newsprint, boards, and a weight, to dry.

tip To find the center of the spine cloth, pinch the cloth lightly at the top and bottom, wrong sides together.

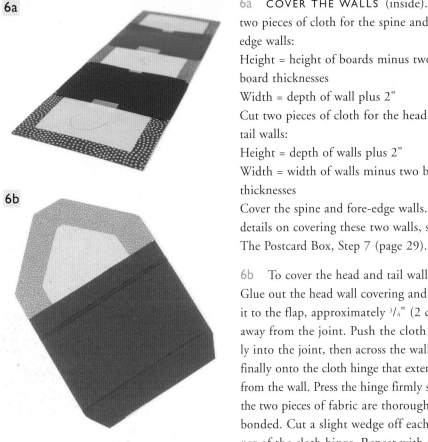

6a COVER THE WALLS (inside). Cut two pieces of cloth for the spine and fore-edge walls:

Height = height of boards minus two board thickness

Width = depth of wall plus 2"

Cut two pieces of cloth for the head and tail walls:

Height = depth of walls plus 2"

Width = width of walls minus two board thicknesses

Cover the spine and fore-edge walls. For details on covering these two walls, see The Postcard Box, Step 7 (page 29).

6b   To cover the head and tail walls: Glue out the head wall covering and apply it to the flap, approximately ³/₄" (2 cm) away from the joint. Push the cloth firmly into the joint, then across the wall, and finally onto the cloth hinge that extends from the wall. Press the hinge firmly so that the two pieces of fabric are thoroughly bonded. Cut a slight wedge off each corner of the cloth hinge. Repeat with the tail flap.

7a ATTACH THE RIBBON TIES. To determine the placement of your ribbons, make a pattern out of a piece of paper cut to the height of the cover board. Place this pattern on the outside of the cover and pierce the cover board with your awl or potter's needle. These pinpricks are your guide marks for chiseling. Before chiseling, protect your table top with scrap board. Select a chisel that is the width of your ribbon. Place the chisel on the guide mark and chisel (from the outside in).

7b   Thread the ribbons into the slits (about ¹/₂" (1 cm)). On the inside, peel away a thin layer of board just deep enough to accommodate each ribbon.

Glue the ribbon (using undiluted PVA) and sink it into the excavated area. Press down and burnish with your folder. Repeat these steps to attach ribbons to the base board.

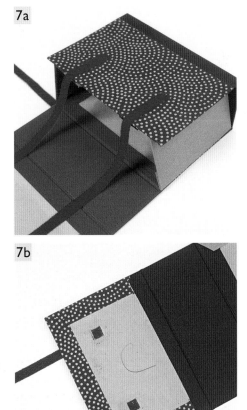

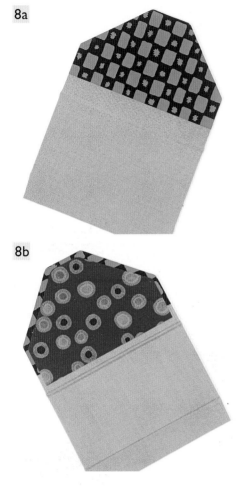

8a

8b

8a LINE THE HEAD AND TAIL FLAPS.
Cut two pieces of paper to line the head
and tail flaps:
Height = height of boards minus two board
thicknesses
Width = width of boards minus two board
thicknesses (adjust if necessary)

8b Before pasting these two papers, fit
them to the angled flaps and trim off the
excess paper. Paste out these papers (one at
a time) and apply them to the appropriate
panels. Rub down with your bone folder,
through a protective waste sheet. Put the
flaps aside to dry between waste sheets,
under a board and weight.

**9a ATTACH THE HEAD AND TAIL
FLAPS TO THE CASE.** Sharply crease the
hinge against the wall, to form a right
angle. Place a flap, right side up, on a
waste sheet. With a stiff piece of waste
paper, mask the area to be kept glue free.
Using undiluted PVA, glue out the hinge.
Take care to stay one board thickness
away from the wall with your glue brush.

9b Center the hinge on the base board,
and press down well. Make sure no glue
has squeezed out and stained the wall.
Keep your micro-spatula handy, should
you need to remove excess glue. Repeat
with the other flap.

10 LINE THE CASE. Remember that
when pasted, paper will expand in width,
anywhere from a hair to a full $1/4$" (.5 cm)
depending on the paper and the adhesive.
Trim accordingly. The measurements
below are approximate.

Cut three pieces of paper, to line the cover,
base and fore edge flaps:
Height = height of boards minus two board
thicknesses
Width = width of boards minus two board
thicknesses (adjust if necessary)

Paste out these papers (one at a time) and
apply them to the appropriate panels. Rub
down with your bone folder, through a
protective waste sheet. Sandwich the box
between sheets of dry newsprint; place
under boards and a weight, until dry.
Note: Changing the newsprint sheets
speeds up the drying process.

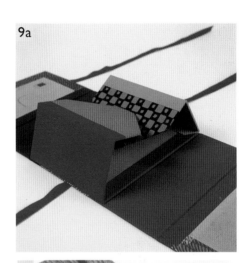

9a

9b

Some photographs, such as these four of a sweet boy named Nicholas, are meant to be displayed rather than hidden away in albums. The Picture Frame Box is a wonderful way to celebrate a specific event—a birth, a graduation, a marriage. A cross between a book and a box, this extended case unfolds, accordion-style, to reveal the four photographs framed within. Make the interior as decorative as possible, and freely mix other mementos, such as birth announcements or fragments of letters, in with the photographs. My preferred covering material is a specific Japanese paper called Momi, *which has the strength and the folding qualities of cloth.*

picture frame box...

memories of a special child

MATERIALS	Two-ply museum board, for mats	Decorative papers (mats)	Grosgrain ribbon
	Binder's board, for case	Decorative papers (linings)	Mylar
	Momi paper	Two bone clasps (also called *tsume*)	Glue, mixture and paste

getting started:
cutting the boards and windows

- Cut the museum board to make four mats. Cut board to desired height and width. Make sure grain runs parallel with the spine edge.
- Cut out the windows in the mats. The windows should be approximately ¹/₂" (1 cm) smaller in both height and width than the photos.

ABOUT MOMI PAPERS These papers are tough enough to be substituted for fabric, but they require special handling. The beauty of these color-saturated papers is in their crinkly surface. If the paper becomes too relaxed—for example, by the application of paste—the crinkles flatten out and the wonderful texture is lost. The solution to this problem is threefold: (1) use mixture instead of paste; (2) apply the mixture to the board rather than to the paper; and (3) don't be too aggressive with your bone folder.

I

2a

2b

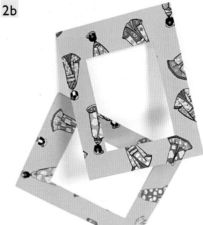

I Cover the mats. Cut four pieces of decorative paper:

Height = height of mat plus 1 ¹/₂" (4 cm)
Width = width of mat plus 1 ¹/₂" (4 cm)

2a **PASTE OUT THE PAPER.** Center the mat on the paper and press into place. Cut the corners and finish the edges. (see The Basics, page 22). To finish the interior of the mat, make two diagonal cuts, from corner to corner, through the paper in the windows. Remember that wet paper tends to tear when being cut. If your paper is saturated with paste, give it a few minutes to dry before cutting.

2b Prior to pasting these flaps into position on the back of the mats, trim away excess paper with your scissors. Paste. Place the covered mats between sheets of newsprint, and under a board and a weight until dry.

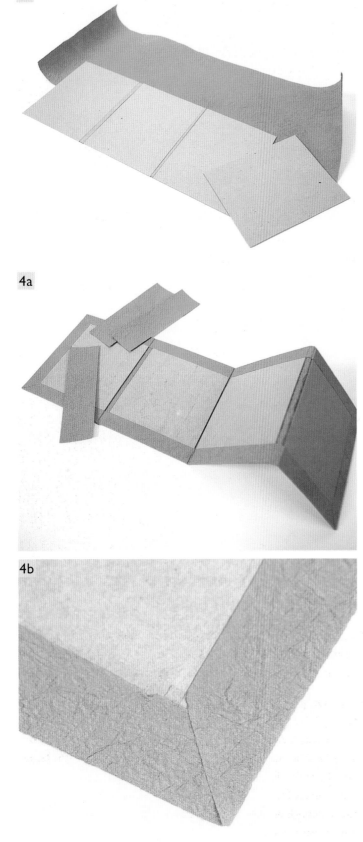

3   **CUT THE BOARDS FOR THE CASE.** Cut four pieces of binder's board:

Height = height of mats plus two board thicknesses

Width = width of mats plus two board thicknesses

From your scrap board, cut two joint spacers. Different spacers are required because, as the accordion closes, the first and the last joints must accommodate more bulk than the middle joint.

Spacer 1 (for first and last joints) = two binder's board thicknesses plus two mat thicknesses plus $^1/_{16}$" (.15 cm)

Spacer 2 (for middle joint) = two binder's board thicknesses

4a   **CONSTRUCT THE CASE.** Cut a piece of Momi paper large enough to accommodate the four case boards and the joint spacers. Add a $^3/_4$" (2 cm) turn-in allowance around all four edges. Brush mixture onto the case boards and gently press them into position on the paper, leaving the proper joint spaces between the boards. Cut the corners (see The Basics, page 22). Applying your mixture sparingly, glue the head turn-in.

4b   Bring the paper onto the boards and, with the edge of your bone folder, gently press the paper into the three joints. Pinch in the paper at the corners. Repeat with tail turn-in. Complete the spine and fore edge turn-ins.

CUT THREE HINGE STRIPS FROM THE MOMI PAPER.
Height = height of case boards minus $^1/_4$" (.5 cm)
Width = 2" (5 cm)

Stipple the mixture onto one hinge strip and, centering this strip, gently press the paper into the joints and onto the boards. Repeat with the other two hinges. Put the case aside to dry, flat, under a light weight.

5a

5b

5c

5d

5a   ATTACH THE BONE CLASPS.
Position the four mats on the case and close the case. Thread the ribbons through the slits in the bone clasps and place the clasps in the desired location on the front of the case. Mark the front of the case with four pinpricks, one on each side of the two clasps directly below their slits. (To make sure the clasps end up level with each other, make all marks on a pattern and then transfer these marks to your case.) Open up the case, remove the mats, and place the case right side up on a scrap board. Select a chisel to match the width of your ribbons.

Holding the chisel vertically, make four parallel chisel cuts (two per clasp), starting at the pinpricks and chiseling downward.

5b   Angle the ends of two short pieces of ribbon and push down through the cuts, to form receiving loops for the clasps. Slide the clasps into the loops. Adjust the ribbons for a snug fit. Guide the main ribbons to the back of the case; mark for their insertion (again, with a pinprick or pattern). Make one vertical slit per ribbon.

5c   Adjust the ribbons to make them taut. (Be sure the mats are inside the case

as you make these adjustments.) On the inside of the case, spread the ribbon ends in opposite directions.

5d   With your knife, trace the outline of the ribbons, cutting and peeling up a shallow layer of board. Glue the ribbons into these recesses, using undiluted PVA. Make it as smooth as possible.

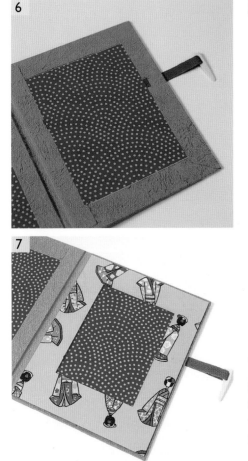

6

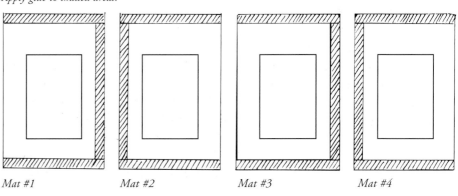

8

6 LINE THE CASE. Cut four pieces of decorative paper to fit within the case turn-ins. Paste out the papers and apply them to the case. Press the case, between newsprint and boards, under a light weight.

7 ATTACH THE MATS. The mats are glued to the case along three edges; the fourth edge is kept unglued, to allow for the insertion of the photographs. Glue backs of mats as follows (see diagram):

Mat 1: Glue out the head, tail, and the long edge of the mat that will sit near the outer edge of the case (i.e., away from the joint). Use undiluted PVA, masking off areas of the mat to be kept glue free with narrow strips of scrap paper. Brush the glue approximately $^{1}/_{2}$" (1 cm) onto the mats. Center the mat on the case board, pressing down along the edges with your bone folder. Carefully scoop away any seeping glue with a micro-spatula.

Mats 2 and 3: Glue out the head, tail, and the long edge of the mat that will sit near the middle joint. Continue as with mat 1.

Mat 4: Follow the process as with mat 1.

When all four mats have been glued to the case, press the case by placing it between newsprint and boards, and under a light weight.

8 CUT FOUR PIECES OF MYLAR, approximately 1" (3 cm) smaller than the mats in both height and width. Slide the Mylar under the mats. Insert photos under the Mylar.

Apply glue to shaded areas.

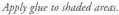

Mat #1   Mat #2   Mat #3   Mat #4

Tip: How to Back Fabric

MATERIALS

Cloth (lightweight cotton, handkerchief linen, silk)

Japanese tissue, such as mulberry paper

Paste (thick!)

Water, in a spritzer bottle

It is thrilling to transform special fabrics—a piece of a wedding dress, a quirky 1930s cotton print, an old silk scarf—into bookcloth. The method is simple, involving a bowl of paste and a sheet of Japanese paper. In contrast to the whimsically patterned silk used here, the case was lined with discarded pages from a botanical book found at a flea market.

1. Test your fabric for permanency of dyes. Wet a small piece. If the colors run, stop! Check out alternative backing techniques, such as those involving heat-set tissues.

2. Cut away the selvage from the fabric.

3. Cut a piece of Japanese tissue approximately 1" (3 cm) larger than the fabric on all four sides. Make sure the grain direction of fabric and paper is the same.

4. Place the fabric, right side down, on a non-porous surface (glass, Formica, Plexiglas). Spritz the cloth with water until it is fully saturated. Straighten the grain and smooth away wrinkles.

5. Paste out the sheet of Japanese tissue.

6. Hold a ruler over the short edge of the pasted paper, approximately 1/2" (1 cm) and parallel with that edge. Give the ruler a quick press onto the paper. You are, briefly, pasting the ruler to the paper so that when you pick up the ruler the paper will adhere to it and be easily lifted off your workbench.

7. Lift and position the paper (pasted side down) on the fabric and slowly lower it onto the material. Don't place it down all at once, or you will trap huge air bubbles.

8. Draw a stiff dry brush across the surface of the paper, pressing to ensure a tight bond and to remove air bubbles.

9. Paste out the four edges of the paper that extend beyond the edges of the fabric. Stick down, onto one of these edges, a small piece (1"–2"; 3–5 cm) of heavyweight paper. This will become a lifting tab when the fabric has dried.

10. Carefully peel the backed fabric off your workbench and reverse it onto a drying surface. (Keep a sheet of Plexiglas in your studio for just this purpose. It can be put aside while the fabric is drying and not occupy valuable workbench space.) Make sure the four pasted edges are well adhered to the surface.

11. When the fabric has dried, slide the micro-spatula behind the paper tab and peel the fabric away from the board. Wash the drying surface with warm, soapy water.

The first scrapboard I ever saw was in a wonderful painting by the American trompe l'oeil master John Frederick Peto (1854–1907). A simple board crisscrossed with ribbons, it held letters and other ephemera and was an enchanting precursor to the modern bulletin board. My desk-sized version, encased in a portfolio, is a celebration of Victorian design. The bookcloth is embossed with a floral pattern, the ribbon is extravagant, and the tiers of pockets are cut from sheets of hand-marbled papers.

the victorian scrapboard...

organize your memories

MATERIALS

Binder's board
Bristol board (10 point)
Decorative paper; one
sheet 19" by 25"

(48 cm by 64 cm) is suffi-
cient for the scrapboard
pictured here
Bookcloth

Ribbon
PVA and mixture
Pressure-sensitive
adhesive (roll)

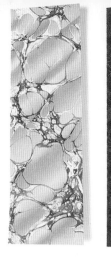

- Collect the memorabilia for your scrapboard:
  letters, birth announcements, cards.
- Gather the decorative materials for your box.
  These can include decorative paper, ribbon,
  or swatches of fabric for pockets.

1a

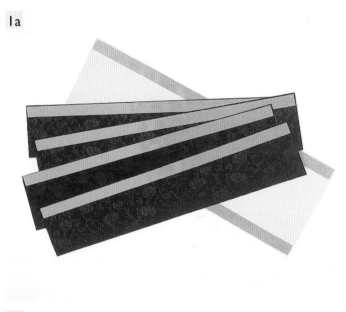

1a   CONSTRUCT THE SCRAPBOARDS.
Cut two pieces of binder's board to the
desired height and width. My boards are
12" by 10 ¹/₂" (30 cm by 27 cm).

Cut decorative paper into eight strips:
Height = 4" (10 cm) (adjust this measurement to accommodate pockets of different
depths)
Width = width of boards plus 2" (5 cm)

Cut bookcloth into six strips:
Height = 2¹/₂" (6 cm)
Width = width of boards plus 2" (5 cm)

Apply strips of pressure-sensitive adhesive
to the right side of the bookcloth, along
one long edge. Do not peel up the paper
backing. Apply strips of pressure-sensitive
adhesive to the wrong side of the decorative
paper, along both long edges. Do not peel up
paper backing. Apply a strip of pressure-
sensitive adhesive to the entire width of the
lower (tail) edge of each board. Do not
peel up paper backing.

1b

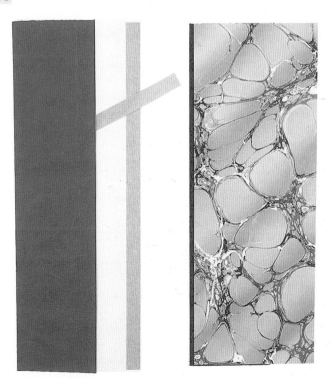

1b   Adhere the decorative papers to the
bookcloth strips. Peel off the backing
paper from one edge of the decorative
paper. Press the paper onto the cloth,
approximately ¹/₈" (.3 cm) away from the
edge of the cloth without adhesive on it.
Roll back the paper, peel off the backing
strip from the cloth, and press the paper
onto the cloth. Repeat with the other five
strips. If your cloth tends to unravel, dip a
finger into the PVA and run it along the
exposed edge of cloth, sealing it. **Note:** The
photos illustrating Step 2 are of small scale
models of the actual scrapboards.

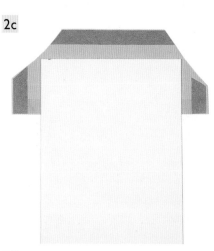
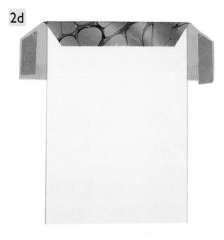

2a ASSEMBLE THE SCRAPBOARDS.

Place one of the two reserved decorative papers face down on the workbench. Remove the adhesive backing from the lower edge. Position the right side of the board (the side with the adhesive strip along its tail edge) on the paper, centered left to right and approximately 1" (3 cm) down from the head. Press.

2b Cut the corners, staying 1 1/2 board thicknesses away from the tip of the board.

2c Apply adhesive to the two side (spine and fore-edge) turn-ins.

2d Bring the head turn-in onto the board and pinch in the corners.

2e Press the two side turn-ins onto the board.

2f To attach the first pocket, mark the board for its placement. Peel off the backing strip and stick down the pocket. Repeat with the second pocket. To adhere the third pocket, mark for its placement, remove the backing strip from the lower board edge, and stick down the pocket.

2g Turn the board over and complete the turn-ins. Starting with the upper pocket, apply strips of adhesive to the two side turn-ins; press them onto the board. Repeat with the second pocket. At the third pocket, first cut the corners and then bring in the long (tail) turn-ins before the two side ones.

2h–i Repeat Step 2 to complete the second scrapboard.

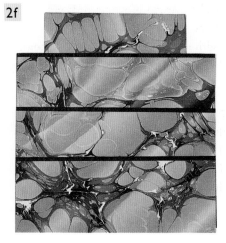

NEXT   CUT OUT THE CASE UNITS.
The case is composed of three parts: front
and back, made of binder's board; and
spine, cut from the flexible (bristol) board.
There is no joint spacer. Pay attention to
the grain direction which runs, as always,
from head to tail.

CUT THE FRONT AND BACK CASE BOARD:

Height = height of scrapboards plus $1/4$"
(.5 cm)

Width = width of scrapboards plus $1/4$"
(.5 cm)

CUT THE SPINE PIECE:

Height = height of scrapboards plus $1/4$"
(.5 cm)

Width = thickness of the two scrapboards
plus two (case) board thicknesses plus two
cloth thicknesses, plus $1/8$" (.3 cm)

CUT THE BOOKCLOTH:

Height = height of case boards plus $1 1/2$"
(4 cm)

Width = width of case boards, laid out,
plus $1 1/2$" (4 cm)

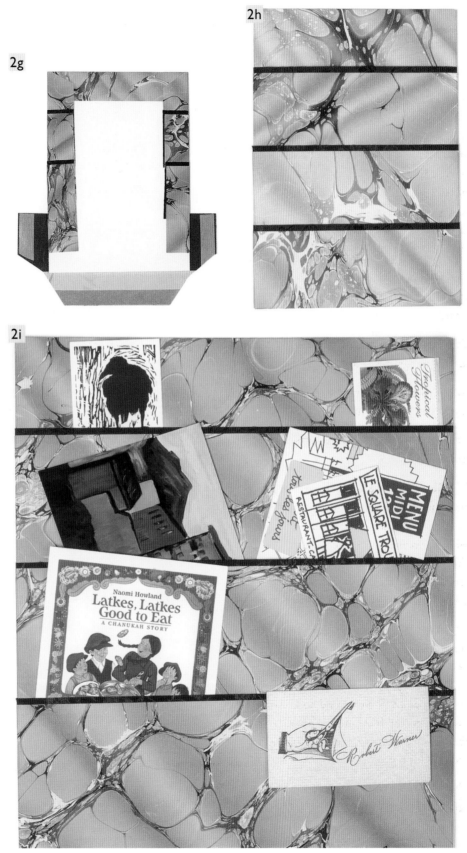

Make a pattern to determine the placement of the ties. Place the case, right side up, on a protected work surface. Transfer your placement mark to the case, and chisel. Repeat on the back board.

4b   Push the ribbons, with the help of your micro-spatula, through the slits and glue them into place.

3   **CONSTRUCT THE CASE** by gluing out the boards and adhering them to the cloth (see drawing). Cut the corners and complete the turn-ins (see The Basics, page 22).

Cut a hinge strip from the bookcloth:
Height = height of scrapboards
Width = width of spine piece plus 2" (5 cm)
Apply mixture to the cloth, center it on the spine, and press it firmly into place. Use your bone folder to sharply impress the edges of the case boards through the cloth.

Fill in the case. Cut two pieces of scrap paper large enough to fill in the area of exposed board on the inside of the case. Apply mixture to these papers and adhere them. This will counterbalance the pull of the boards toward the outside of the case. Put the finished case aside to dry, between newsprint sheets, under pressing boards and a weight.

4a

4b

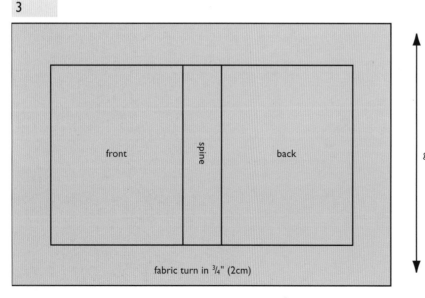

3

front

spine

back

grain

fabric turn in ³/₄" (2cm)

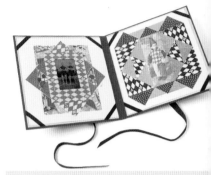

5

5 GLUE THE SCRAPBOARDS TO THE CASE. Apply undiluted PVA to the wrong side of a scrapboard. Remove excess glue from the edges. Center the board on the case board and press it into position. Hold it for a minute or two, until the glue begins to set. Put newsprint, a pressing board, and a weight on top. Repeat these steps to attach the second scrapboard, making sure the pockets on both boards are facing in the same direction.

LEAVE THE FINISHED CASE under weights for several hours.

Ribbons can be used as fairly minimal corner restraints. They could also be glued diagonally, from side to side, across the entire surface of the board, creating the pineapple pattern in Peto's depictions.

No glue! No paste! No complicated cuts! This box is, simply, two pieces of paper joined at the base with strips of pressure-sensitive adhesive. Since it is such an austere construction, The Paper Box needs a paper with character and body to give it charm. If the color is vibrant, this spunky box needs very little ornamentation: A button or two and a piece of bright thread are enough. The paper used here is a lustrous handmade. Its linen content gives the paper both strength and tactility. In this project you will use a new technique: scoring paper. This is a simple but important technique (see The Faux Book Box for an additional application), and deserves the highlighting starting on page 49.

the paper box...
for the love of paper

MATERIALS

A good-quality hand-made paper

Thread

Buttons

Elastic cord

Pressure-sensitive adhesive on a roll

PVA

getting started:
cutting the first piece of paper

- Cut out the first piece to the following dimensions:

  Height = height of object to be boxed (referred to as "object" hereafter)

  Width = width of object, plus twice the thickness of the object, plus 2"–4" (5–10 cm), depending on the size of the box.

- If you intend to sew through the spine and fore-edge walls (as in the box pictured), increase this width measurement by approximately ¼" (.5 cm) since the stitching on the inside of the box juts into the base, diminishing its overall width.

ONE

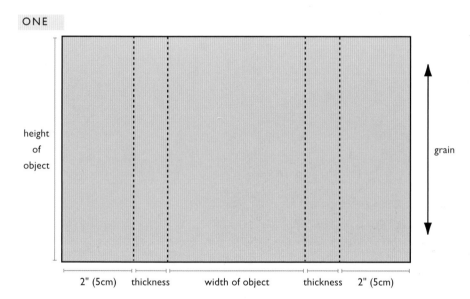

height of object · grain

2" (5cm) · thickness · width of object · thickness · 2" (5cm)

HOW TO SCORE A PIECE OF PAPER

Place a sheet of blotter, or a pad of newsprint, on your workbench. To make deep, crisp score marks, you must work on a cushioned surface.

Mark the paper for scoring. To mark, make small pinpricks with a sewing or potter's needle. (If you make pencil markings, you will need to erase them later.)

Place your triangle on the paper. The right angle of the triangle must sit on top of the pinprick. Draw a line with your bone folder, from the marked edge to its opposite edge (head to tail; spine to fore-edge). Keeping the triangle in place, scoot under the paper and run your folder up and down, pressing the paper firmly against the edge of the triangle. Remove the triangle. Fold over the paper and sharpen the crease with your folder.

Note: Steps 2 through 8 and Step 10 are illustrated with scale models of the actual box.

1 SCORE THE PAPER by centering the object on the paper and making two pin-pricks, to the left and right of the object, on the tail edge of the paper. Score and sharply crease the paper. (See How to Score a Piece of Paper on page 49.)

2 FORM THE SPINE AND FORE-EDGE WALLS. Measure the thickness of the object and transfer this measurement to your paper, with pinprick markings, to the outside of the previously scored lines. (To measure for thickness, see The Basics, page 16.) Score and sharply crease the paper. Round the sharp corners, at head only.

3 CUT OUT THE SECOND PIECE:
Height = three times the height of the object plus twice its thickness
Width = width of object enclosed in the first piece
Grain must run from spine to fore-edge.

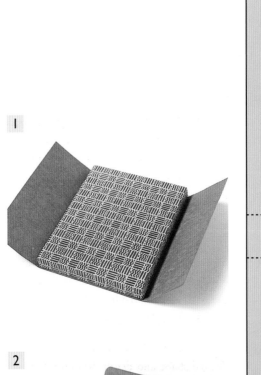

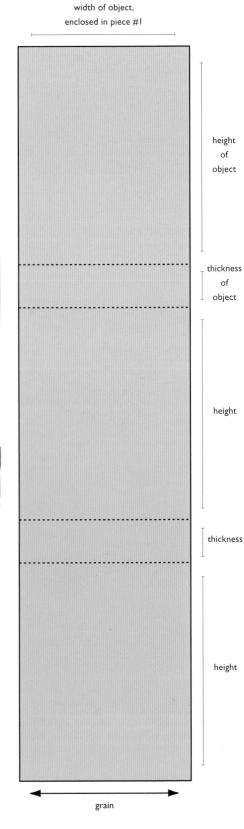

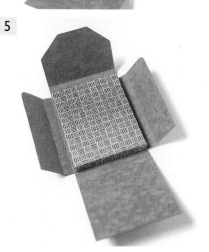

4 SCORE THE PAPER by centering the (enclosed) object on the paper and making two pinpricks, to the top and bottom of the object, on the spine edge of the paper. Score and sharply crease the paper.

From the head and tail walls. Measure the thickness of the object to be enclosed and transfer this measurement to your paper, with pinprick markings to the outside of the previously scored lines. Score and sharply crease the paper.

5 TRIM HEAD AND TAIL FLAPS to desired shape and depth. Round off all sharp edges on head flap.

6a SEW ON BUTTON AND APPLY REINFOCEMENT PATCHES. Decide on the placement of the buttons and elastic cord on the head and tail flaps. Punch holes.

6b Before sewing, cut and glue small patches of paper over punched area, either inside or out. Insert cord and sew on buttons.

7a

7b

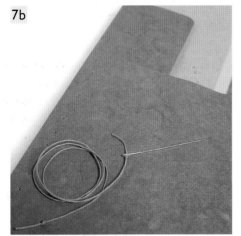

7c

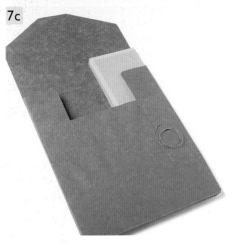

7a, b, c   If sewing the spine and fore-edge walls, punch holes through the tail flap, the flanges under the flap, and through corresponding areas on the spine and fore-edge walls. (See Tip on page 53.) Do not sew.

8

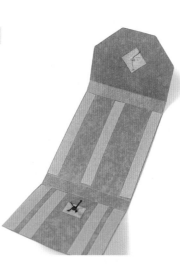

8a

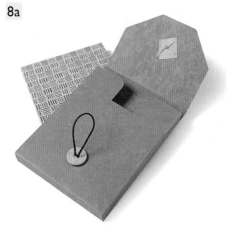

8   **ATTACH THE TWO UNITS** by applying strips of pressure-sensitive adhesive to the second piece, in the areas illustrated.

8a   Peel off backing paper on the base area only, and stick the two units together. If omitting decorative stitching, peel off backing paper on the tail flap and carefully align this flap with the spine and fore-edge flanges; press down into place.

8b   If sewing, thread two needles. Start on the inside of the tail flap, and sew toward the head in an overcast stitch, sewing up both sides simultaneously. When the sewing is complete, sneak inside and peel off backing paper on tail flap; press the flap onto the flange.

There are many ways to close this box. Apply ribbon ties, as in previous projects. Use adhesive-backed Velcro dots. Or, cut a slit in the tail flap and insert head flap into this slit.

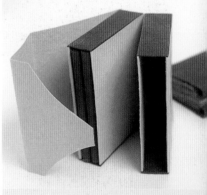

HEDI KYLE *Demosta*
5" x 4³/₈" x 2¹/₂"
(13cm x 11cm x 6cm) (closed)

books: Firenze paper soaked in coffee
box: Tim Barrett handmade and Moriki papers

Tip *How to Punch Holes*

Make a punching block by taping scrap boards together, to the depth of your walls and to the appropriate height. To punch holes through the tail flap and the flanges underneath, insert this block into the box, align the papers in the proper position, and punch through both papers simultaneously. I held a ruler ¹/₄" (.5 cm) away from the edge of the tail flap and punched holes at ¹/₂" (1 cm) intervals. To make sure the holes in the two walls are in the corresponding positions, move the right angle of a triangle from hole to hole, punching holes in the wall as you go from head to tail.

The inspiration for this box is a poignant object from centuries ago. Made when the possession and reading of Tarot cards was a dangerous pursuit, this box was built to deceive. The titling on the spine is a clue to the contents, but the craftsmanship of this small beauty manages to hide its secrets. My box holds a collection of cards of another sort. In France, April Fool's Day is celebrated with fish: chocolate fish, pastry fish, paper fish. "Poissons d'Avril" fill this box.

The Faux Book Box is comprised of two units: An inner scored paper container and an outer case. If you intend to make the spine of your box resemble an old book, choose the covering material carefully. Select a strong but flexible handmade paper, and paint or stain it to look like leather. Accept the crinkles that will inevitably develop as the paper is molded over the fake raised bands. They are suggestive of a well-used, much-loved object.

the faux book box...
memories of second-hand bookshops

MATERIALS

For the scored container:
- A good-quality medium-weight paper
- Decorative paper
- Paste
- Pressure-sensitive adhesive on a roll

For the case:
- Binder's board
- Strong, flexible handmade paper (spine)
- Decorative paper
- Bristol board, 10 point
- Headbands (optional)
- Cord
- PVA, mixture and paste

getting started:
select the paper for the laminate

- Cut one piece of medium-weight paper and two pieces of decorative paper to the same dimensions:
  Height = height of object to be boxed, plus two thicknesses of object, plus 1" (3 cm)
  Width = twice the width of the object, plus one thickness of object, plus 1" (3 cm)
- Make sure the grain runs from head to tail on all three papers.

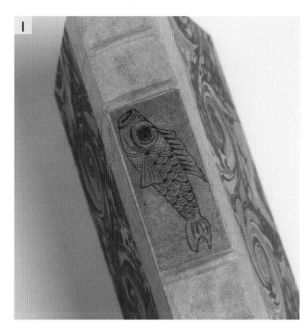

1

1 PREPARE THE LAMINATE
to become the scored-paper container. Dampen the plain paper with a wet sponge. Paste out the decorative papers (one at a time) and apply one to each side of the dampened paper. Press out air bubbles with your hands. Place this laminate between dry newsprint sheets, sandwich it between pressing boards, and leave it under weights for half an hour.

Cut the laminate to the following dimensions.

Height = height of object plus a hair, plus two thicknesses of object.
Width = twice the width of object, plus one thickness of object.

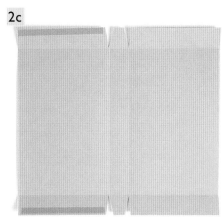

2d

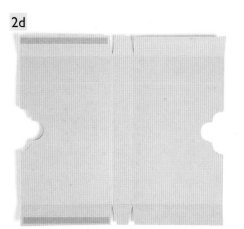

2e

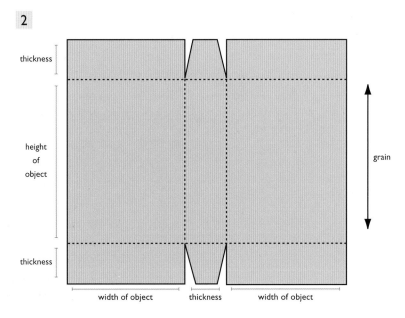

2f

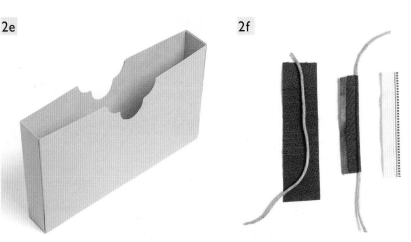

2 CONSTRUCT THE PAPER CONTAINER. The laminate *must* be scored while it is still damp. If it is dry, the against-the-grain folds are cracked and flaky. When using expensive materials, make a prototype out of cheap paper then transfer the measurements to the laminate.

2a Following the procedure for scoring paper described in The Paper Box (page 49); score the laminate.

2b Cut away triangular wedges.

2c On the left-hand panel (inside), apply strips of pressure-sensitive adhesive close to the outer edges of the head and tail turn-ins. Repeat on the right-hand panel, applying the adhesive to the reverse (outside) of the laminate.

2d Make thumb cuts on the fore-edges, of desired size and design.

2e Fold up the box and stick the turn-ins together, tucking the spine tab in between the two long turn-ins.

2f Optional: Glue endbands (available from bookbinding suppliers, or made by gluing fabric around a piece of cord) to head and tail, at spine. The bands are cut to the exact thickness of the box spine.

2

thickness

height of object

thickness

grain

width of object   thickness   width of object

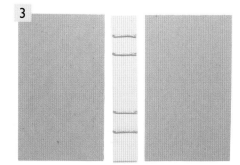

3 CUT OUT THE CASE BOARDS.
The front and back boards are cut from binder's board:
Height = height of box, plus two board thicknesses
Width = width of box, plus one board thickness
The spine is cut from 10 point bristol board:
Height = height of box, plus two board thicknesses
Width = thickness of box, plus two (case) board thicknesses, plus slightly more than two spine paper thicknesses
Optional: To make fake raised bands, glue strips of cord across the spine board, at desired intervals. If you plan to label your box, space these bands accordingly.

4 CUT OUT THE COVERING MATERIALS. Cut one piece of strong but thin and resilient handmade paper to cover the spine:
Height = height of boards, plus 1 1/2" (4 cm)
Width = desired width—from front board, across spine, to back board
Cut two pieces of decorative paper to cover the boards:
Height = height of boards, plus 1 1/2" (4 cm)
Width = distance from edge of spine paper to fore-edge of board plus 1" (3 cm)

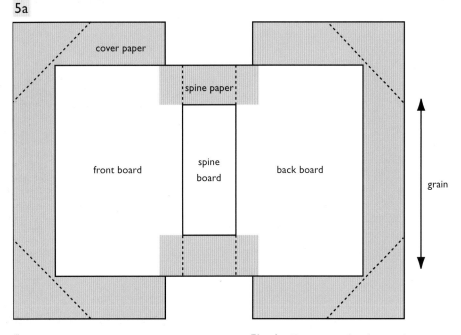

cover paper

spine paper

front board

spine board

back board

grain

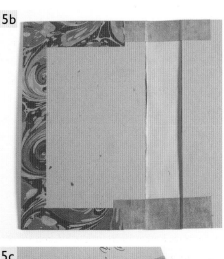

5b

5c

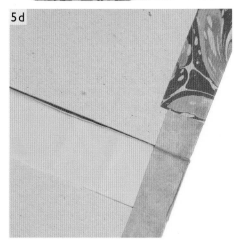

5d

5 ASSEMBLE THE CASE
(see diagram.)

5a Paste out the spine paper. Center the spine piece (cord side down) on the paper. Flip the spine over onto a piece of wax paper. Mold the paper around the cords, sliding the paper down from the head and tail to provide ample material to stretch around the cords. Moisten the paper with a sponge and continue to work it around the cords with your bone folder, until the hubs are well-defined. Turn the spine over, onto a piece of newsprint, and re-apply paste to the head, tail, and spine extensions. Place the front and back boards on the paper, snugly abutting the spine board. Bring in the head and tail turn-ins. Turn the case over and carefully try to smooth out the wrinkles. Don't be too obsessive: They are inevitable and they contribute to the old-book look.

5b–d Paste out the decorative papers and apply them to the boards. These papers should overlap the spine paper by a small margin. Cut the corners and finish the edges (see The Basics, page 22).

Cut the inner hinge strip from the spine covering paper:
Height = height of paper box
Width = width of case spine board, plus 2" (5 cm)

Do not paste this strip to the case.

6 ATTACH THE BOX TO THE CASE.
Glue the spine of the box with undiluted PVA, taking care not to stain the end-bands. With your finger, remove any excess glue. Stick the right side of the hinge strip onto the spine, centering it head to tail and left to right.

6a, b Rub it down well. Paste out the entire back of the hinge strip and center the box on the spine of the case. Use your bone folder to force the hinge sharply against the spine edges of the case boards. Press the paper onto the boards. Keeping the box in an upright position, fill it with scrap boards cut to fit. This will help press the box to the case.

NEXT LINE THE CASE. Cut two pieces of decorative paper:
Height = height of paper box
Width = width of case boards, minus two board thicknesses
(Remember to anticipate the stretch of the paper in width, and trim it a bit narrower if necessary.)

Paste out these papers and apply them. With the case remaining in this open position, stack newsprint, pressing boards and weights on top of each board, and let dry.

7 LABEL THE BOX. Using a pen, paintbrush, rubber stamp or computer, generate artwork for the label. Draw or print it on a contrasting paper. Paste the label to the spine, between the bands.

6a

6b

7

VARIATION

The marbled paper used on this box is a contemporary Italian marble based on a traditional pattern. Old book papers can also be retrieved and reused on new book and box projects. Scavenge around second-hand bookstores for discarded covers. Take them home and let them soak in a bathtub filled with warm water. As the adhesive dissolves, the papers will loosen and peel away from the boards. If this doesn't happen, keep adding hot water to the bath, and gently pull the papers away from the boards. Remove the papers and blot them with paper towels. Place them right side up on wax paper (in case of a sticky residue). Sandwich the papers between blotters, pressing boards, and weights until dry.

If the papers seem too fragile for re-use, paste them onto sheets of Japanese tissue while still damp, and press as above.

Sometimes, the best surprises are the unexpected ones. As the marbled papers float off the boards, printed "waste sheets"—magazine pages, handwritten account-book pages, a sheet of music—appear below. Used as board liners, these sheets can also be retrieved with additional soaking time.

Creative ideas—whether watercolor paintings or sketches for a new craft project—deserve a special home. You won't find a more wonderful home for your work than The Artist's Portfolio.

And just as the artwork deserves a special place, so does your portfolio deserve a label. Labels enliven objects, identify their contents, and help to distinguish the fronts from the backs. In this case, the artist is a wonderful calligrapher, Anna Pinto. To protect the paper label, cut away several layers of the cover board, creating a well into which the label can be dropped. The cutaway area is slightly larger than Anna's artwork. The result is a shadow that frames the artwork.

The Artist's Portfolio consists of a case with three separately constructed flaps. Keep the outside plain, to highlight the unique contents. But there is a surprise when you open this box: Here is one portfolio that will never be mistaken for a standard art-supply-store item.

the artist's portfolio...
preserve your memories

MATERIALS	Binder's board (case)	Bookcloth	PVA, mixture and paste
	Museum board, two or four ply (flaps)	Decorative paper	Artwork for cover
		Ribbon	

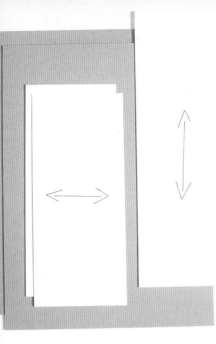

getting started:
cutting the boards

- Cut out the front and back case boards:
  Height = height of material to be boxed, plus ¹/₂" (1 cm)
  Width = width of material to be boxed, plus ¹/₄" (.5 cm)
- Cut out the boards for the flaps:
  Head and tail flaps: cut two
  Height = 4" (10 cm), or desired height
  Width = width of material to be boxed, plus ¹/₈" (.3 cm)
  Fore-edge flap: cut one
  Height = height of material to be boxed, plus ¹/₄" (.5 cm)
  Width = 4" (10 cm), or desired width, matched to height of
  head and tail flaps
- Grain should run from head to tail on all boards.

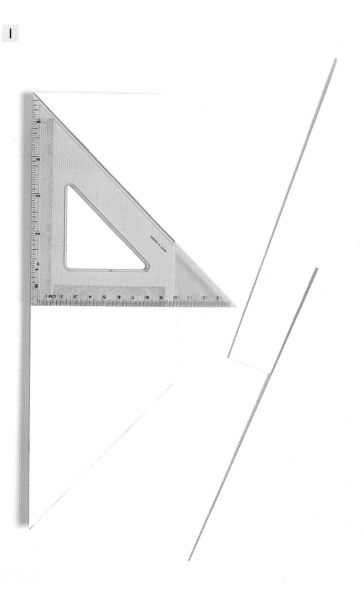

|

MITER THE CORNERS of the flaps. Using a 45-degree triangle, draw and cut off one wedge from each head and tail flap, and two wedges from the fore-edge flap.

2a–f **CONSTRUCT THE FLAPS.**
For the head and tail flaps, cut two pieces of cloth:
Height = height of board, plus the thickness of the material to be boxed, plus 1 ³/₄" (4.5 cm)
Width = width of board, plus 1 ¹/₂" (4 cm)
For the fore-edge flap, cut one piece of cloth:
Height = height of board, plus 1 ¹/₂" (4 cm)
Width = width of flap, plus the thickness of the material to be boxed, plus 1 ³/₄" (4.5 cm)
Glue out the boards using mixture and stick them onto the cloth. *Pay attention: The head and tail flaps are mirror images and must be glued in opposite orientations.* Note that the untrimmed long edge of each board sits near a generous cloth extension. This cloth—the thickness of the material to be boxed, plus 1" (3 cm)—will eventually become the walls of the portfolio and the hinge attachment of the flaps to the case.

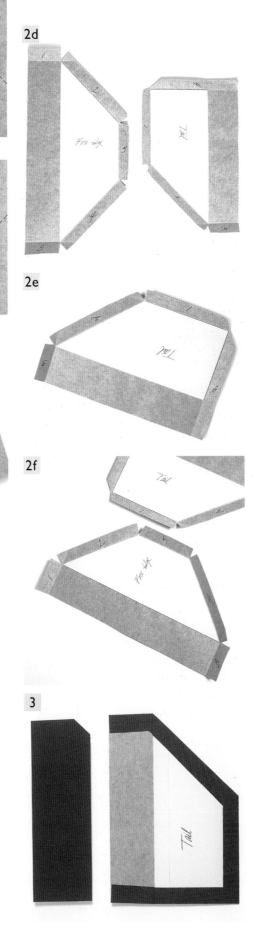

2a ³/₄" (2 cm)   ³/₄" (2 cm)

Head

³/₄" (2 cm)

Thickness of material to be boxed, plus 1" (3 cm)

2b Tail

2c

2d Free edge   Tail

2e Tail

2f Free edge

3 Tail

Trim cloth near the angled edges of the boards, as illustrated, to create the usual ³/₄" (2 cm) turn-in. Cut corners and finish all edges except the long edge, which will become the hinge attachment to the case. To cleanly cover the angled edges of the flaps, remove triangular bits of cloth. Crease and re-crease the turn-ins in all possible sequences to determine which bits to cut. When cutting, end cuts 1 ¹/₂" board thicknesses away from the boards. Glue the turn-ins in the labeled sequence.

3   CUT THE INNER HINGE STRIPS for all three flaps. For the head and tail flaps, cut two strips of cloth:

Height = thickness of the material to be boxed, plus 1³/₄" (4.5 cm)

Width = width of flap, minus two board thicknesses

For the fore-edge flap, cut one strip of cloth:

Height = height of flap, minus two board thicknesses

Width = thickness of the material to be boxed, plus 1³/₄" (4.5 cm)

Before gluing, place the hinge strips in the proper position on the flaps, and cut off the corners that extend beyond the angled edges. With pencil, mark each flap approximately ³/₄" (2 cm) away from its long edge. Apply mixture to the hinge strips (one at a time). Starting on the ³/₄" (2 cm) markings, press the cloth onto the board. Push the cloth sharply against the board edge with your folder. Press the extending cloth onto the fabric below. Don't stop pressing until the two are well bonded. Sandwich this hinge between newsprint, pressing boards, and weights until dry. To even out the raw edges of this hinge extension, trim a uniform amount of cloth off each of the three flaps.

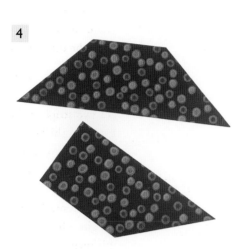

Spacer #1 (flaps)

4   LINE THE FLAPS. Cut two pieces of paper to line the head and tail flaps:

Height = height of board, minus two board thicknesses

Width = width of board, minus two board thicknesses

Cut one piece of paper to line the fore-edge flap:

Height = height of board, minus two board thicknesses

Width = width of board, minus two board thicknesses

Before gluing, place the lining papers in the proper position on the flaps and cut off the corners that extend beyond the angled edges. Apply adhesive to the papers and stick them down. Put flaps aside to dry, between newsprint sheets and under boards and a weight.

5   FORM THE FLAP WALLS. From your scrap board, cut a strip equal to the thickness of the material to be boxed; this is your wall spacer (Spacer 1). To form the head, tail, and fore-edge walls, push this spacer firmly against the long edge of each flap and crease the fabric hinge to form a right angle. On the head and tail flaps only, trim a wedge off the cloth hinge near the spine edge. Put the flaps aside.

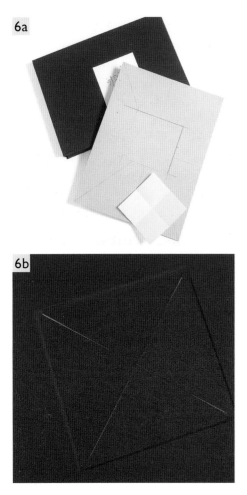

6a

6b

6a CONSTRUCT THE CASE.

Decide on the placement of the cover artwork. Cut and peel away layers of board equal to the thickness of the artwork (See Tip on page 66). Cut the spine spacer from a strip of scrap board. The width of this spacer is the thickness of the flap spacer, plus two (case) board thicknesses, plus the thickness of one flap, plus two cloth thicknesses.

Cut a piece of bookcloth to cover case:
Height = height of boards, plus 1 1/2" (4 cm)
Width = width of boards laid out with spacer in place, plus 1 1/2" (4 cm)
Glue out the front board. Draw away excess glue with your brush from around the edges of the label recess. Make sure that no small bits of cardboard are stuck to the surface. Place this board on the left-hand side of the cloth, centered on height and with a 3/4" (2 cm) margin on your left. Press the board down. Turn the cloth over immediately and, working through a sheet of scrap paper, press out all air bubbles with your folder. Find the edges of the cut-away area and shape the cloth sharply against these edges.

6b If your cloth is stubborn and refuses to stretch, cut an X in the middle of the recessed area; start and end the cuts approximately 1/4" (.5 cm) away from the corners. As you shape the cloth against the edges, be careful not to smear the glue. Once shaped, flip the case over, place the spine spacer next to the cover board, glue out the back board, and put it down. Press, then remove the spacer and turn the case over. Press the cloth down well, working first with your hands and then with your folder. Flip the case back to its original position, cut the corners, and finish the edges (see The Basics, page 22).

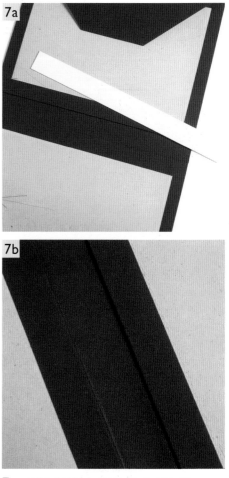

7a

7b

7 CUT AND APPLY THE SPINE HINGE STRIP.

7a Cut a piece of cloth:
Height = height of case minus 1/4" (.5 cm)
Width = width of spine spacer plus 2" (5 cm)
Apply mixture to this hinge and center it on the spine.

7b Rub vigorously, forcing the fabric against the board edges. Trim a hair off the spine spacer in width, and re-position it in the spine area. With a weight on top, it will press both cloths together. Let sit for half an hour to one hour.

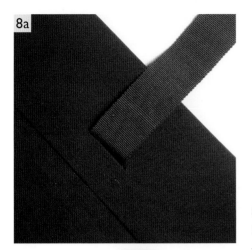

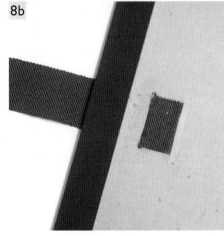

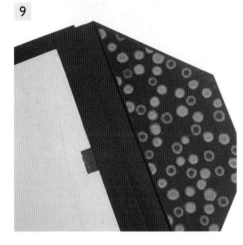

8a ATTACH THE RIBBON TIES.
Decide on the placement of the ties. (If you wish to center them, cut a scrap of paper to the height of the case and fold it in half. Voila! The center.) Mark this area with a pinprick. Select a chisel the width of your ribbon. Chisel, vertically, from the outside of the case. Be sure to protect your tabletop before chiseling. Repeat on the back board.

8b Insert the ribbons into these slits and pull them to the inside of the case. Cut and peel up a shallow layer of board and glue the ribbon ends with undiluted PVA, sinking them into the recess.

9 GLUE THE FLAPS TO THE BACK OF THE CASE. Use undiluted PVA, and start with the fore-edge flap. Masking the walls with a piece of scrap paper, glue out the hinge. Remove excess glue, taking care not to smear glue onto the wall area. Center the flap by height on the case; it should sit just inside the board edge of the case. Press down well with your folder. Repeat with the head and tail flaps, positioning the flaps flush with the spine edge of the case. To reduce bulk at the outer corners where the head and tail flaps overlap the fore-edge flap, miter the corners after gluing. To miter, make a diagonal cut through both hinges simultaneously, drawing the knife from the right angle formed at the outer overlapping area to the right angle formed at the inner overlapping area. You will need to peel up the head and tail flaps slightly, to remove the triangular wedge from the fore-edge flap underneath. Re-apply a dot of adhesive, if necessary, and stick back down.

NEXT **LINE THE CASE.**
Cut two pieces of paper:
Height = height of case, minus two board thicknesses
Width = width of case, minus two board thicknesses
The lining for the back board might need to be trimmed; check the fit before gluing. Apply adhesive to these papers and stick them down. Place newsprint, boards, and weights on the case, and let sit until dry.

NEXT **APPLY ARTWORK TO COVER.**
Apply appropriate adhesive to artwork, and stick down into cover recess. Remember to anticipate the expansion of wet paper, and trim accordingly. When setting in a photograph or artwork involving water-based inks, use a moisture-free (pressure-sensitive) adhesive.

Tip: How to Prepare a Cover Board for a Label

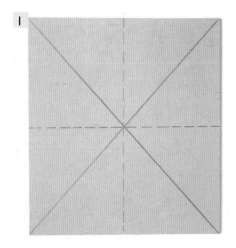

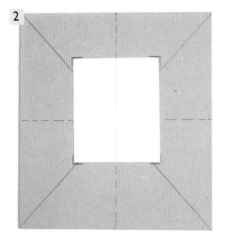

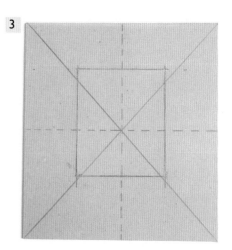

1. Cut a paper pattern:

Height = height of artwork, plus ¹/₈" (.3 cm)

Width = width of artwork, plus ¹/₈" (.3 cm)

(The pattern is larger than the artwork to allow for a shadow around it once it is glued into place.) Crease this pattern in half, both vertically and horizontally, to find the center.

NEXT Draw diagonal lines, from corner to corner, on your cover board. Using your triangle to maintain right angles, draw a line from head to tail, through the bisecting point. Draw a second line, from spine to fore-edge, through the bisecting point.

2. Place the paper pattern on the board, aligning its creased lines with the drawn lines. Slide the pattern up and down and side to side to decide on the placement of your artwork. Or keep it right where it is at dead center.

NEXT Trace the outline of the pattern on the board.

3. Using your triangle and a knife with a sharp blade, cut through the pattern's lines. Make several cuts over the same area before proceeding from one line to the next.

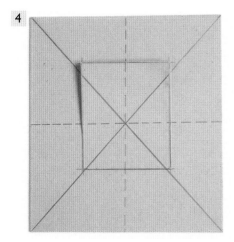  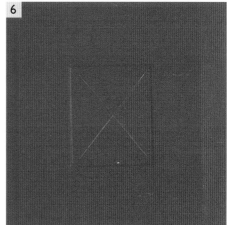

4. Use the tip of the blade to dig under and lift up the board in one corner. Grab this corner and peel up several layers of board with the help of the knife. Peel and lift in the direction of the grain. Clean up the corners by scraping with your knife. Make sure the edges are crisp.

NEXT Smooth the cut-away surface by rubbing vigorously with your folder. Also smooth down the roughed-up outer edges of the cut-away.

5. Glue out the board and position it on the cloth. Flip the board over and immediately find the edge of the recess with your hands. (Work through a newsprint sheet to protect the surface of the cloth.) Work out all air bubbles, puncturing the cloth with a sewing needle, if necessary. Shape the cloth sharply against the edges of the recess with a tapered bone folder.

6. If the cloth is stubborn and refuses to mold itself against the edges of the cut-away, make two diagonal slits through the cloth, starting and ending the slits at least $1/8$" (.3 cm) away from the corners.

Its charm is in its size (2¹/₂" [6 cm] square), as well as in its materials. Several small boxes, stacked or scattered, have more presence than one large and lonely box. So make lots of boxes—and let them become your jewels!

The Jewelry Box consists of two units: a four-walled tray and a case. The case extends slightly beyond the edges of the tray, creating a small lip. Once assembled, the front of the case becomes the hinged lid of the box.

Keep in mind the rules of boxmaking: Wherever hinging occurs, use cloth instead of paper. The one exception is in the use of Momi papers (please see my note in The Picture Frame Box on page 37). If not using these resilient Japanese papers, I use bookcloth for the case construction. In the directions, the case material is referred to as cloth.

the jewelry box...
memories of treasures and trinkets

MATERIALS			
	Binder's board	Cloth or paper (tray)	Ribbon
	Museum board, two ply (liners)	Cloth or Momi paper (case)	PVA, mixture and paste
		Bone clasp	

getting started:
cutting the boards

- Cut out the boards for the tray following the layout shown.
- Pay attention to the logic of the cuts, which ensures that all parts sharing the same measurements are cut in sequence, and with a minimum of marking.
- Base:

  Height = desired height of tray, plus two covering thicknesses

  Width = desired width of tray, plus two covering thicknesses
- Head and tail walls:

  Height = desired depth of tray, plus one board thickness

  Width = desired width of tray, plus two covering thicknesses
- Spine and fore-edge walls:

  Height = height of base board, plus two board thicknesses

  Width = desired depth of tray, plus one board thickness

Ia

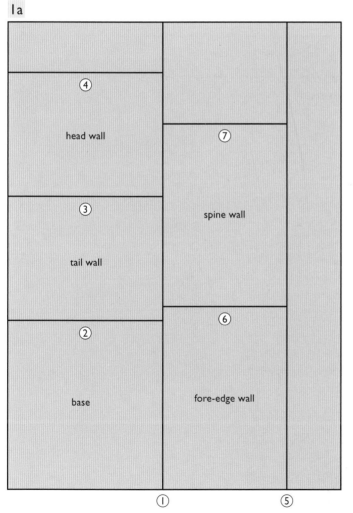

④

head wall

③

tail wall

②

base

⑦

spine wall

⑥

fore-edge wall

① ⑤

grain

Ib

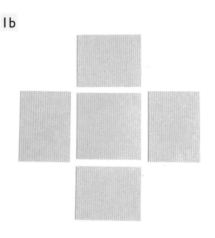

Ic

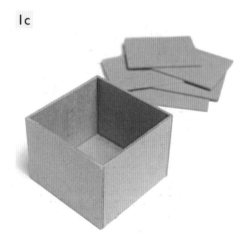

Ia–c **CONSTRUCT THE TRAY**
(see The Basics, page 20.) Glue the walls in the proper sequence: head, fore-edge, tail, spine.

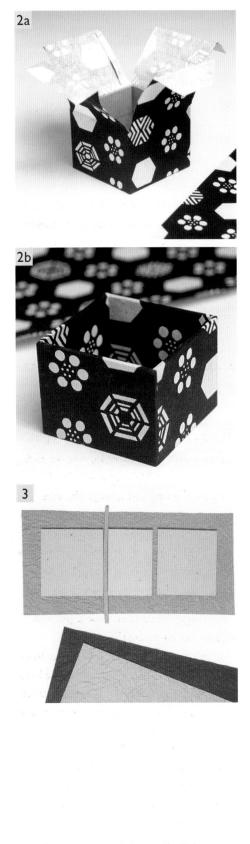

2a COVER THE TRAY. Cut out the covering material, a strip twice the depth of the tray plus 1 1/2" (4 cm), and long enough to wrap around all four walls plus 1/2" (1 cm). If the material is too short to wrap around the tray in one continuous strip, piece together two shorter strips, making sure that the seam falls on a corner of the tray.

2b Cover the tray (see The Basics, page 20).

3 CUT OUT THE THREE CASE BOARDS to the following dimensions. Remember that the grain must run from head to tail on all boards.
Front and Back:
Height = height of tray, plus two board thicknesses
Width = width of tray, plus one board thickness
Spine:
Height = height of tray, plus two board thicknesses
Width = depth of tray (Here's an easy and accurate way to get this measurement: Sharply crease a small piece of scrap paper to form a right angle; place the tray on top of this paper and push the tray snugly into the right angle; make a second, parallel crease, over the top of the tray. The distance between these two crease marks is the exact depth of your tray.)

From your scrap board, cut a slender strip a scant two board thicknesses in width. This will be used as a spacer when gluing up the case.

NEXT **CUT OUT THE CASE CLOTH** or Momi paper:
Height = height of boards, plus 1 1/2" (4 cm)
Width = width of boards, laid out with joint spacer plus 1 1/2" (4 cm)

4 CONSTRUCT THE CASE. Glue out the front board and place it on the cloth, approximately 3/4" (2 cm) away from all three edges. Press into place. Position the spacer against the spine edge of the board, glue the spine piece, position the spine on the cloth, and push it firmly against the spacer. Remove the spacer and place it on the other side of the spine. Glue the back board, position it on the cloth pushed firmly against the spacer, and press into place.

5 CUT THE CORNERS and finish the edges (See The Basics, p. 12). Cut the inner hinge cloth:
Height = height of the tray
Width = width of case spine, plus 2" (5 cm)
Grain, as always, runs from head to tail. Cut shallow triangular wedges off all four corners of this cloth.

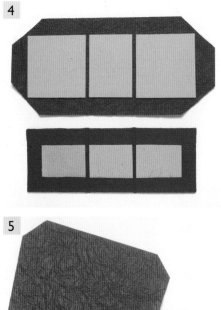

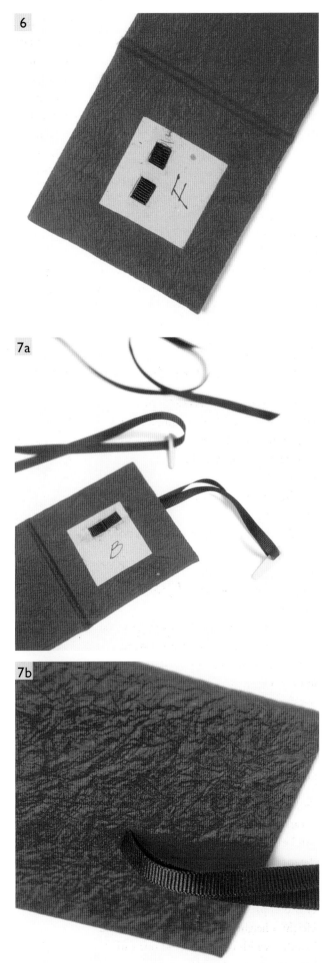

6 GLUE OUT THE HINGE CLOTH, center it on the spine, press the cloth firmly into the joints of the case with your bone folder, then onto the front and back case boards. Rub down well.

7a ATTACH THE BONE CLASP. Feed the ribbon through the slit in the bone clasp. Place the tray in the case, close it, and position the bone clasp on the front of the case, in its desired location. (If making more than one box, prepare patterns for the placement of the ribbons on both front and back.) Mark the front of the case with two pinpricks, one on each side of the clasp directly below its slit. Remove the tray and arrange the case right side up on a piece of scrap board. Select a chisel to match the width of your ribbon. Holding the chisel vertically make two parallel chisel cuts, starting at the pinpricks and chiseling downward.

7b Angle the ends of a short piece of ribbon and push the ribbon down through the cuts to form a receiving loop for the clasp. Slide the clasp into the loop. Pull the ribbon ends snugly on the inside of the case. Guide the main ribbon to the back of the case; mark for its insertion and make one vertical slit. Feed both ends of the ribbon into this slit, and make the ribbon taut. On the inside of the case, spread the ribbon ends in opposite directions. With your knife trace the outlines of the ribbons, cutting and peeling up a shallow layer of board. Glue the ribbons into these recesses using undiluted PVA. Bone down this area well to make it as smooth as possible.

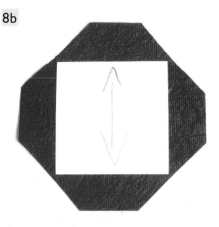

NEXT **ATTACH THE TRAY TO THE CASE.** Spread undiluted PVA onto the bottom of the tray; wipe away excess glue. Place the tray on the back case board. The spine edge of the case should be flush with the spine edge of the tray. Center the tray by height. This placement allows a small lip around the head, fore-edge, and tail. Hold the tray in position for a few minutes, until the glue begins to set. (Take care to keep the tray centered—it's quite a slippery creature at first!) Invert the case, place a board and hefty weight on top, and press for at least a half hour.

Spread undiluted PVA onto the spine wall of the tray; wipe away excess glue. Roll the tray onto the case, spine walls touching; slide a board and a weight into the tray, and press until dry.

8   LINE THE BOX.

8a   If lining with a medium or heavy-weight paper, cut two pieces of paper to the same dimensions. (Remember to anticipate the stretch of the paper across the grain, and to cut it a bit narrower in width.)
Height = height of interior of tray, minus two paper thicknesses
Width = width of interior of tray, minus two paper thicknesses
Paste the papers and apply them to the bottom of the tray and the inside of the box lid. Press until dry.

8b   If lining with a thin or fragile paper or with cloth, first "card" the material around lightweight boards, following the procedure below.
Cut out two pieces of museum board:
Height = height of interior of tray, minus $^1/_{16}$" (0.15 cm)
Width = width of interior of tray, minus $^1/_{16}$" (0.15 cm)

8c   Cut out two pieces of covering paper:
Height = height of boards, plus $1^1/_2$" (4 cm)
Width = width of boards, plus $1^1/_2$" (4 cm)
Paste the papers, center the board on the papers, cut the corners and finish the edges (see The Basics, page 22).

Glue out one board with undiluted PVA and carefully lower it into the tray. Press until it takes hold. If your box is large, place newsprint, a board and a weight on top, and let sit for half an hour. Glue out the second board, and center it on the box lid. Press until it takes hold. Weight and let sit for one half to one hour.

Tip: *How to Make a Ribbon from Bookcloth*

1. Cut a piece of bookcloth a scant $^3/_4$"
(2 cm) in width and twice the desired length,
plus 2" (5 cm). Grain must run lengthwise.
Use your spring divider to divide this strip
into $^1/_4$" (.5 cm) increments (lengthwise).

2. Score the fabric into thirds. To score,
position the cloth wrong side up on a piece
of blotter. Working against a metal straight-
edge with a tapered bone folder, "draw"
two parallel lines $^1/_4$" (.5 cm) apart from
head to tail. Crease the fabric firmly along
these score lines.

3. With your small brush, apply mixture to
the cloth, starting in the middle of the fabric
and working the adhesive toward the ends.
Do not over glue. Turn the edges of the strip
in toward the center of the fabric—first one,
then the other—pressing with your fingers
as you go. Place the strip between two waste
sheets and press well with your bone folder.
Let sit, between pressing boards and under
weights until ready to use.

To close this little brocade box, make
a ribbon from book cloth. This is an
elegant alternative to store-bought
ribbon when using bone clasps as
closures on an all-cloth project.

My mother's button "box" was actually a large glass jar filled to the brim with a glorious mixture of buttons. When we were sick we sorted the buttons by color and size. When well, and playing pirates, we poured buttons over the carpet and reveled in our "pieces of eight." In homage to that jar, The Button Box is a true treasure chest full of plastic bounty. It even depends on buttons for its finial and feet embellishments. The Button Box is composed of a four-walled tray mounted on a platform, and a removable lid.

the button box...
memories of once-treasured garments

MATERIALS	Binder's board	Ribbon	PVA, mixture and paste
	Museum board, two-ply	Buttons	Epoxy or wood glue
	Assorted decorative	Thread	(optional)
	papers		

getting started:
cutting the boards

- Cut out the boards for the tray, following the layout below.
- Base:

  Height = desired height of tray, plus two covering thicknesses

  Width = desired width of tray, plus two covering thicknesses
- Head and tail walls:

  Height = desired depth of tray, plus one board thickness

  Width = desired width of tray, plus two covering thicknesses

  (same as width of base board)
- Spine and fore-edge walls:

  Height = height of base board, plus two board thicknesses

  Width = desired depth of tray, plus one board thickness

  (same as height of head and tail walls)

1a–c   CONSTRUCT THE TRAY
(see The Basics, page 20). Glue the walls in the proper sequence: head, fore-edge, tail, spine.

1a

1b

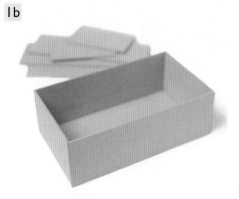

1c

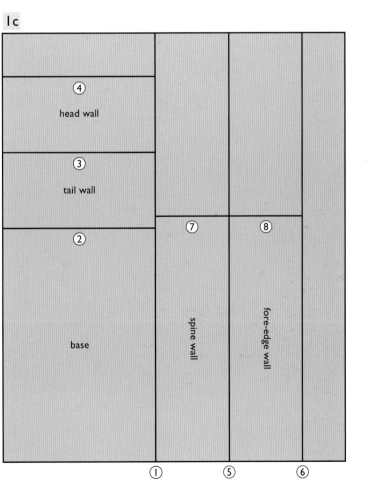

(4) head wall

(3) tail wall

(2) base

(7) (8)

spine wall

fore-edge wall

(1)   (5)   (6)

grain

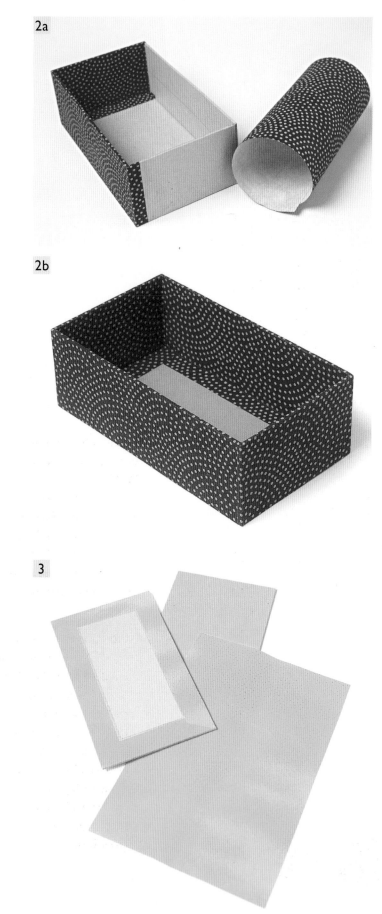

2a

2b

3

2 COVER THE TRAY.

2a Cut out the covering paper, a strip twice the depth of the tray plus 1 $^1/_2$" (4 cm), and long enough to wrap around all four walls plus $^1/_2$" (1 cm). If the paper is too short to wrap around the tray in one continuous strip, piece together two papers, making sure that the seam falls on a corner of the tray.

2b Cover the tray (see The Basics, page 21).

3 CONSTRUCT THE LID AND THE BASE PLATFORM. Cut out two boards to the same measurements:

Height = height of tray, plus two board thicknesses
Width = width of tray, plus two board thicknesses
Cut two pieces of decorative paper to the same measurements:
Height = height of boards, plus 1 $^1/_2$" (4 cm)
Width = width of boards, plus 1 $^1/_2$" (4 cm)
Cover the boards by pasting the papers and centering the boards on them. Cut the corners and finish the edges (see The Basics, page 22). Fill in the exposed area of the board with scrap paper. Put the boards aside to dry between newsprint sheets and pressing boards, and under weights.

4

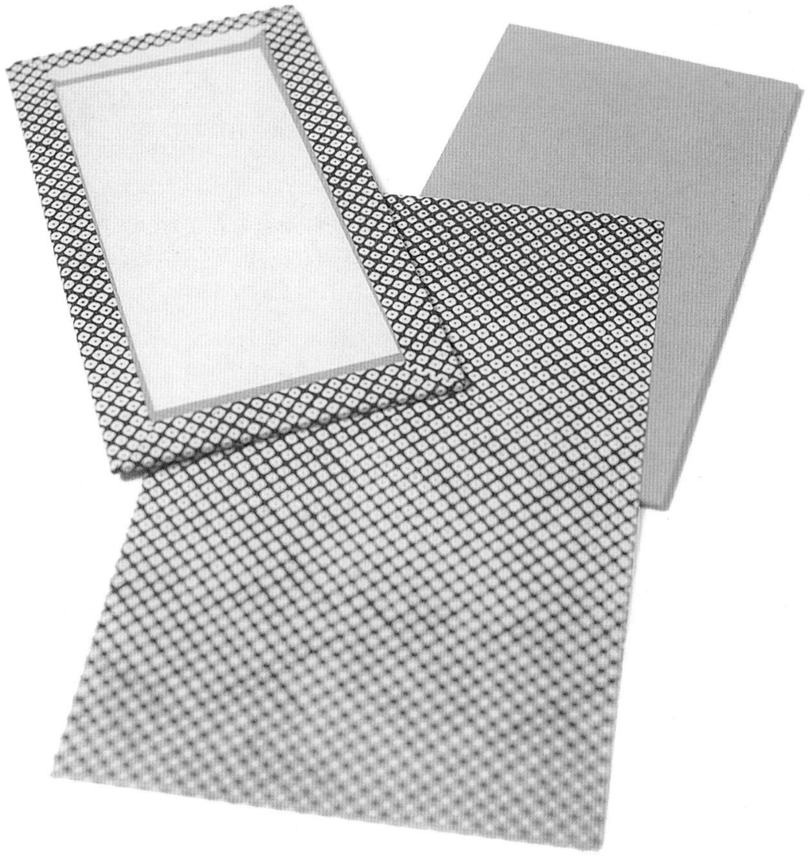

4 CONSTRUCT THE LID LINER. This board, glued to the inside of the lid, keeps the lid anchored to the tray. Cut one board:

Height = height of interior of tray, minus two paper thicknesses

Width = width of interior of tray, minus two paper thicknesses

Cut one piece of decorative paper:

Height = height of board, plus 1 1/2" (4 cm)

Width = width of board, plus 1 1/2" (4 cm)

Cover and fill in this board, following the procedure described above. Put it aside to dry.

5

5 DECORATE THE TRAY. Cut two lengths of ribbon, long enough to wrap around the tray plus 2" (5 cm). Starting 1" (3 cm) in from one end, sew on buttons. Avoid placing buttons where the ribbon folds around the corners. Glue the ribbon with undiluted PVA—one wall length at a time—and stretch it around the tray, pressing with your bone folder as each wall is covered. Hide the raw ends of the ribbons by overlapping and tucking under the leftover bits.

6a

6b

6 FINISH THE LID.

6a Cut, cover and glue together small pieces of board to create an interesting lid. Thread several buttons together to form a finial. Punch holes through all lid layers except for the liner, and sew on the finial. To protect the finial as the liner is being pressed onto the lid, arrange two stacks of small boards, side-by-side with a gap in between the size of the finial and its anchor boards. Invert the lid over this setup. Glue the lid liner with undiluted PVA, wipe off excess glue from the edges, and center this board on the lid. Hold this liner in place for a few minutes, until it stops sliding and begins to set. Place a pressing board and weights on top, and let sit for a half hour to one hour.

6b Glue the tray to the base platform. Apply undiluted PVA to the bottom of the tray. Wipe off excess glue from the edges. Center the tray on the platform and hold in place for a few minutes, until it begins to set. Invert the tray and place a pressing board and a heavy weight on top. Let sit for a half hour to one hour.

7   LINE THE BOX and attach the feet. If sewing buttons (feet) to the base plat-form, punch holes and sew on buttons before lining the box. If gluing buttons with either epoxy or wood glue, attach buttons after lining the box. Cut a piece of two-ply museum board just large enough to fit inside the tray, with a little breathing room. Cut a piece of covering paper:

Height = height of board, plus 1 1/2" (4 cm)
Width = width of board, plus 1 1/2" (4 cm)
Paste out the paper and center the board on it. Cut the corners and finish the edges (see The Basics, p.22). Press briefly. Glue the wrong side of this board with undilut-ed PVA, wipe away excess glue from its edges, and drop the liner into the tray. Hold for a few minutes until the glue begins to set. Put a scrap board (cut to fit) and weights in the tray, and let sit a half hour to one hour.

7

This is indeed a sweet container, and a versatile one as well. It can hold a single piece of chocolate or a ton of St. Valentine's Day cards. The Candy Box, like the prototypical Whitman's Sampler, consists of two nesting trays. Because this is a simple project—the second tray is an exact repeat of the first—it is a good candidate for multiples. To make an edition of three small boxes instead of one requires just a few more minutes in cutting time, an extra hour or two in construction time, and a couple of dollars more in materials. Be brave: produce an edition!

A survey of vintage candy boxes reveals yards of embossed, gilt, and lace papers. For my edition, I likewise selected a textured, brilliant red paper. The boxes are lined with antique tea chest paper—paper used in Japan to wrap bricks of tea.

the candy box...
memories of fudge and friendships

MATERIALS	Binder's board	Decorative paper
	Bristol or museum board for linings	PVA, mixture and paste

getting started:
cutting the boards for the tray

- Cut out the boards for the inside tray, following the layout shown.
- Base:

    Height = desired height of box, plus two paper (covering) thicknesses

    Width = desired width of box, plus two paper (covering) thicknesses
- Head and tail walls:

    Width = desired width of box, plus two paper (covering) thicknesses

    Depth = desired depth of box, plus one board thickness, plus one lining thickness
- Spine and fore-edge walls:

    Height = height of base, plus two board thicknesses

    Depth = desired depth of box, plus one board thickness, plus one lining thickness

la, b   CONSTRUCT THE TRAY

(see The Basics, page 20). Smooth all seams
with a sanding stick.

la

CUTTING LAYOUT FOR ONE BOX

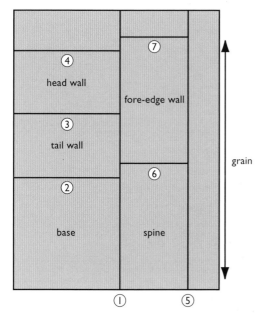

lb

CUTTING LAYOUT FOR THREE BOXES

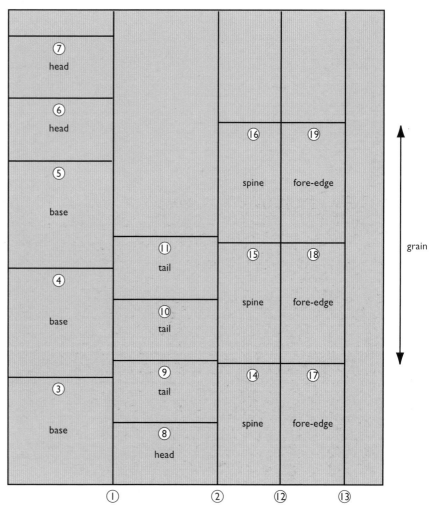

2a, b **COVER THE TRAY.** Cut out the covering paper—a strip twice the depth of the tray plus 1 ½" (4 cm), and long enough to wrap around all four walls plus ½" (1 cm). If the paper is too short to wrap around the tray in one continuous strip, piece together two shorter strips, making sure that the seam falls on a corner of the tray. Cover the tray (see The Basics, page 21).

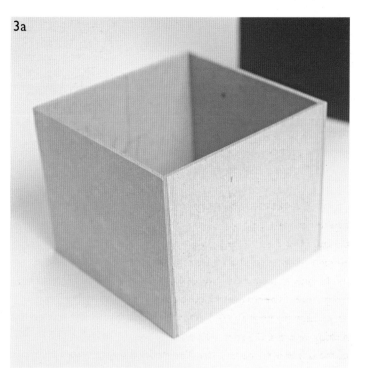

3 CUT OUT THE BOARDS for the outside tray following the layout in Step 1. This tray is slightly larger than your inside tray.

3a To measure for its parts you must use your completed inside tray as a pattern. Place your tray on the squared corner of a piece of board (see page 16).

3b Make sure the grain runs from head to tail on both units, and that the spine and tail of the tray are flush with the squared
corner. Mark for cutting. Cut.
Base:
Height = height of tray plus two paper (covering) thicknesses
Width = width of tray plus two paper (covering) thicknesses
Head and tail walls:
Width = width of tray plus two paper (covering) thicknesses
Depth = depth of tray plus one board thickness
Spine and fore-edge walls:
Height = height of base plus two board thicknesses
Depth = depth of tray plus one board thickness

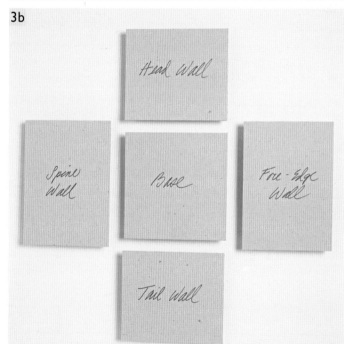

NEXT CONSTRUCT AND COVER THE TRAY (as in Steps 1 and 2).

NEXT CUT OUT THE TWO PLAT-FORMS. These boards are identical in size. They extend beyond the parameters of the larger tray by one board thickness in all four directions. Place the larger tray on the squared corner of a piece of board, flush spine and flush tail. Add two board thicknesses to the height and the width of the tray. This will later be redistributed as a one-board-thickness margin around all edges. Mark and cut out two boards.

4 COVER BOTH PLATFORMS.

Cut out two pieces of decorative paper, larger than the boards by 1 1/2" (4 cm) in both height and width.

4a   Make sure the grain runs from head to tail. Cover the boards, cut the corners and finish the edges (see The Basics, page 22).

4b   Cut two pieces of scrap paper to fill in the remaining exposed board. This filler will balance the board, inducing it to flatten and to adhere more strongly to the tray.

NEXT   **GLUE THE TRAYS** to the platforms. Brush undiluted PVA onto the bottom of the larger tray; wipe excess glue away from the edges. Center the tray on the wrong side of the lid platform. The other platform becomes the base platform. There should be a uniform small extension of a single board thickness beyond the edges of the tray. Hold these two units together for a few minutes, until the tray stops sliding and begins to stick. Flip the box over and place newsprint, a board, and a weight on top of the lid. Keep weighted until dry. Repeat all of these steps with the inside tray. Remember that this tray is smaller than the outside tray. When you are centering the tray on the base platform, the extension of the platform will be larger than one board thickness.

4a

4b

5a

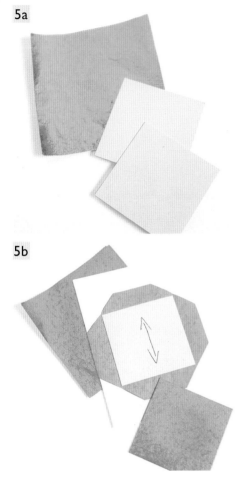

5b

5 LINE THE TRAYS.

5a   If lining the box with a medium or heavyweight paper, cut out two pieces of paper, one to fit inside of each tray. Don't forget to anticipate the stretch of the paper against the grain, and be sure to cut it a bit narrower in width.

5b   Paste out these papers and stick them down. Press, as usual, with newsprint, a board, and a weight, until dry. (If your box is quite small, there is no need to press it.)

If lining the box with a delicate or lightweight paper (such as the gold paper pictured here), it is first necessary to card the paper around boards. Cut out two pieces of lightweight board (bristol or museum board) to the same dimensions:
Height = height of interior of small tray, minus $^1/_8$" (.3 cm)
Width = width of interior of small tray, minus $^1/_8$" (.3 cm)
Cut out 2 pieces of covering paper:
Height = height of boards, plus $1^1/_2$" (4 cm)
Width = width of boards, plus $1^1/_2$" (4 cm)
Cover the boards, cut the corners, and finish the edges. (see The Basics, page 22.)

Apply undiluted PVA to the backs of these boards, wipe away excess glue, and carefully lower the boards into the trays. Hold for a few minutes until the glue begins to set. Cut a piece of scrap board to fit inside each tray. Drop this board into the tray, place a weight on top, and press until dry.

To create a dazzling display of color and pattern, cover the individual parts of the box—trays, platforms, and liners—with a mix of papers.

What is more tender than a ribbon-tied bundle of letters? Pushed to the back of a desk drawer or aban-
doned in a dark closet, they are poignant testimony to friendship and love. They deserve a box of their own.
Here, the letters nestle within a tray; the tray is tucked inside an extended case. The ribbons, besides being
decorative, restrain the letters and also allow their graceful removal from the depths of the tray. The box
closes, seemingly magically, with hidden magnets.

My choice of a textured cloth and a patterned lining paper is not accidental. Because it is difficult
to totally disguise the presence of magnets, lively materials help to distract the eye. The beautiful hand-
painted paste paper, made by Lost Link Design Studio, is based on techniques used in the production of
cover and endpapers in Europe from the late sixteenth through the eighteenth century. A wonderful book
on the subject, originally published in 1942 and still unsurpassed, is Rosamond B. Loring's Decorated
Book Papers (Harvard University Press).

the letter box...
memories of lives past and present

MATERIALS	Bookcloth	Bristol or museum board	Magnetic strips
	Binder's board	Lining paper	PVA, mixture and paste
	(100 point)	Ribbon	

getting started:
cutting the boards for the tray

The goal is a snug fit, with just enough breathing room to allow the ribbons to lift the letters out of the box. To determine the height of the tray, find your tallest letter; to determine width, find your widest letter. Follow the formula below:

- Base:

    Height = height of tallest letter plus $1/8$" (.3 cm)

    Width = width of widest letter plus $1/8$" (.3 cm)

- Head and tail walls:

    Width = width of widest letter plus $1/8$" (.3 cm)

    Depth = $1\,1/2$" (4 cm) or desired depth

- Spine and fore-edge walls:

    Height = height of base board, plus two board thicknesses

    Depth = $1\,1/2$" or desired depth, matched to head and tail walls

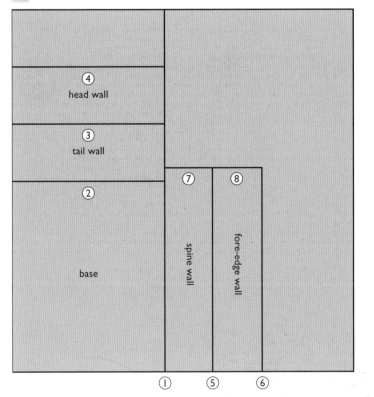

la

④
head wall

③
tail wall

②

base

⑦
spine wall

⑧
fore-edge wall

grain

① ⑤ ⑥

lb

la, b **CONSTRUCT THE TRAY**
(see The Basics, page 20).

2a

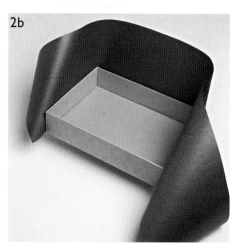

2b

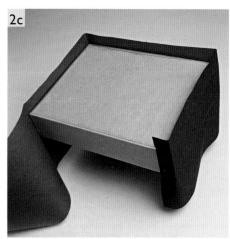

2c

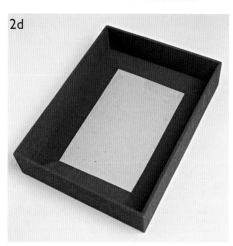

2d

2 COVER THE TRAY.

2a–c   Cut out the covering cloth—a strip twice the depth of the tray plus 1 1/2" (4 cm), and long enough to wrap around all four walls plus 1/2" (1 cm). If the cloth is too short to wrap around the tray in one continuous strip, then piece together two shorter strips, making sure that the seam falls on a corner of the tray.

2d   Cover the tray (see The Basics, page 21).

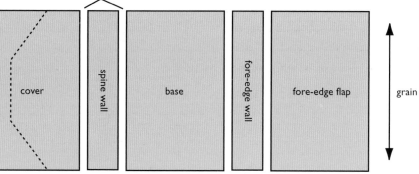

3

space = 2 board thicknesses

cover | spine wall | base | fore-edge wall | fore-edge flap | grain

3 CUT THE BOARDS FOR THE CASE.

Select boards thick enough to accommodate the magnetic strips that will be embedded in the cover and the fore-edge flap (Minimum board thickness: 100 point).

The height is the same for all five case boards:
Height = height of the covered tray, plus two board thicknesses
The width of the boards is the same for the three main panels:

Base = width of tray
Fore-edge flap = width of tray
Cover = width of tray (to be adjusted)
The depth of the walls is as follows:
Fore-edge wall = depth of covered tray, plus a hair
Spine wall = depth of fore-edge wall, plus one board thickness
From your scrap board, cut a slender strip two board thicknesses in width. This will be a joint spacer. See above for a diagram of the board layout.

4

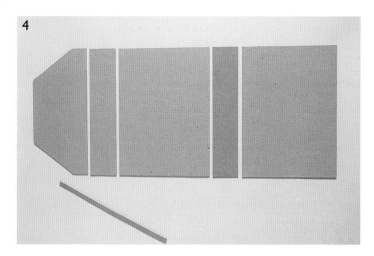

4 **TRIM AND ANGLE** the cover board, as desired. Smooth all sharp edges and corners with a sanding stick.

5a **APPLY THE MAGNETIC STRIPS.** Draw a pencil line $3/4$" (2 cm) away from the angled edge of the cover. Draw a parallel line $1/2$" (1 cm), or the width of your magnet, away from the first line. Cut two magnetic strips to the length of these lines.

5b Cut and peel up a layer of board equal to the thickness of the magnet.

5c Remove the backing paper and sink the magnet into this recessed area. Find the corresponding area on the fore-edge flap for the placement of the second magnet. Be precise because the magnet will not hold unless the two are perfectly aligned.

5d Cut and peel away board. Sink the magnet.

5a

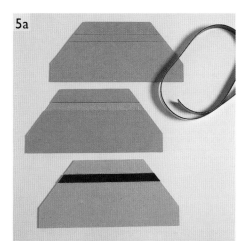

5b

5c

5d

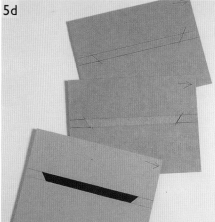

NEXT **CUT THE CLOTH FOR THE CASE:**
Height = height of boards plus 1 1/2" (4 cm) for turn-ins
Width = width of boards laid out, plus joint spacing plus 1 1/2" (4 cm) for turn-ins

NEXT **CONSTRUCT THE CASE.**
Note: When gluing up the case, the cover board is glued magnet side *up* on the cloth; the fore-edge flap is glued magnet side *down*. Glue the boards and apply them to the cloth, working from left to right and using the joint spacer between every two boards. Flip the case over and press down well, eliminating any air bubbles.

NEXT **CUT THE CORNERS** and finish the edges (see The Basics, page 20). As with The Patchwork Box, when dealing with the angled panel you will need to invent a pattern of cuts that allows for the clean coverage of all corners.

6a   COVER THE (INSIDE) WALLS.
Cut two strips of cloth from your leftovers to cover the walls, fill in the joints, and extend onto the three main panels:
Height = height of case minus two board thicknesses
Width = depth of spine wall plus 1 3/4" (4.5 cm)
Make sure, as always, that the grain runs from head to tail.

6b, c   Glue out one strip and position it, centered, on the spine wall. Press it down quickly and work the cloth into the two joints with the edge of your bone folder, moving back and forth between the two joints until the fabric has stuck. Press the cloth onto the cover and base panels. Repeat with the fore-edge wall.

7

7   LINE THE CASE. Cut two pieces of paper to line the cover and the fore-edge flap:
Height = height of case minus two board thicknesses
Width = width of cover and fore-edge flap, minus two board thicknesses
Remember to anticipate the stretch of the pasted or glued paper in width, and cut accordingly. Glue or paste these papers to adhere them. Put newsprint, boards, and weights on these two panels, and let dry.

NEXT **GLUE THE TRAY TO THE CASE.** Cut two pieces of scrap cloth, large enough to fill in (1) the bottom (outside) of the tray; and (2) the base board of the case. Glue them out and stick them down. Using undiluted PVA, paint a thin, consistent layer of glue onto the bottom of the tray. Wipe excess glue from the edges. Position the tray on the base of the case, centered head to tail, and hold until the glue begins to set. Fill with weights, and let dry.

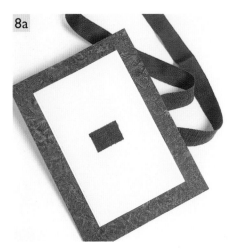

8a

8b

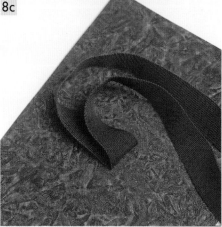

8c

8d

8 ATTACH RIBBONS AND LINE THE TRAY.

8a, b Cut a piece of lightweight board to fit inside of the tray. Allow ¹/₈" (.3 cm) breathing room in both height and width. To cover this board, cut a piece of either paper or cloth to the following dimensions:

Height = height of board plus 1 ¹/₂" (4 cm)
Width = width of board plus 1 ¹/₂" (4 cm)
Adhere the covering material to the board, cut the corners, and finish the edges (see The Basics, page 20). Fill in the back of the board with scrap paper. Select a chisel the width of your ribbons and make a vertical slit through the center of this board.

8c, d Push the ends of two ribbons through the slit and glue down with undiluted PVA on the back of the board. Paint a thin layer of undiluted PVA on this board, wipe off excess glue from the edges, and carefully lower the board into the tray. Keep the ribbons away from the glue. Put a protective waste sheet on top of this liner, fill the tray with boards and a weight, and let dry.

NEXT **GLUE THE CASE WALLS TO THE TRAY.** Brush a thin layer of undiluted PVA onto the spine wall of the tray. Wipe excess glue from the edges. Roll the tray onto its spine wall; fill the tray with weights and press until the spine walls of the tray and case are thoroughly bonded. Repeat with fore-edge wall.

Tip: To Line the Tray with a Framed Photo

Remove the letters from the box and discover an image of the writer—or the recipient—framed beneath. Alter the previous instructions in two places: (1) In cutting out the boards for the tray (Step 1), increase the depth of the walls to accommodate the additional thicknesses of the covered mat and the photograph; and (2) replace Step 12 with the following:

1. Cut two pieces of lightweight board to fit inside the tray. Allow ¹/₈" (.3 cm) breathing room in height and width.

2. Cut a window out of one of the boards. Cut a piece of decorative paper, to cover this mat, to the following dimensions:
Height = height of board plus 1¹/₂" (4 cm)
Width = width of board plus 1¹/₂" (4 cm)

3. Cover the mat, by pasting out the paper and centering the board on the paper. Finish the interior of the mat only (see The Picture Frame Box, Step 2, page 37). Do not cut corners or finish the outer edges.

4. Glue the two ribbons onto the back of the mat.

5. Affix the photo, with pressure-sensitive adhesive, in the proper location on the second (uncut) board.

6. Glue the wrong side of the mat with undiluted PVA to the photo board. Keep the ribbons free of glue. Press.

7. Place the mat, wrong side up, on the workbench. Cut the corners of the paper, staying 1¹/₂ board thicknesses away from the tip of the board. Remember that your "board" consists of the mat, the photo, and the photo board. Re-apply paste to the turn-ins, and adhere them. Fill in the back of the board with scrap paper.

8. Glue the board to the tray by painting a thin layer of undiluted PVA on the board, wiping off excess glue from the edges, and carefully lowering the board into the tray. Put a protective waste sheet on top of the liner, fill the tray with boards and a weight, and let dry.

If you wish to protect the photograph, cut a piece of Plexiglas to the height and width of the two boards, and sandwich it between the mat and the photo board before completing the turn-ins (Step 7).

Ornaments are everywhere! This box, with its flip-top lid and many compartments, can hold collections of all sorts—pens and pen nibs, marbles, costume jewelry, sea shells, special holiday decorations. The Ornament Box is a wonderful vehicle for papers (such as gift wrap papers) too fragile to wrap around the walls of a tray. Cloth does all of the hard work here; decorative papers are pasted on top of the cloth in the final step to give the box its visual punch. I have used an inexpensive Italian Bertini paper because I like its geometric pattern and simple one-color printing. Some of the papers are more typically Florentine, with flourishes and highlights of gold.

The Ornament Box consists of a four-walled tray with partitions and a hinged lid. The lid is actually an upside-down three-walled tray.

the ornament box...

memories of a collector's passions

MATERIALS	Binder's board
	Bookcloth
	Decorative paper
	PVA, mixture and paste

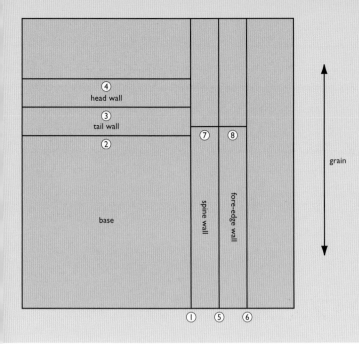

getting started:
cutting the boards for the tray

- Cut out the boards for the tray, following the layout.
- Base:

  Height = desired height of tray, plus two cloth thicknesses

  Width = desired width of tray, plus two cloth thicknesses
- Head and tail walls:

  Height = desired depth of tray, plus one board thickness

  Width = desired width of tray, plus two cloth thicknesses

  (same as width of base board)
- Spine and fore-edge walls:

  Height = height of base board, plus two board thicknesses

  Width = desired depth of tray, plus one board thickness

  (same as height of head and tail walls)

1a, b **CONSTRUCT THE TRAY**
(see The Basics, page 20). Glue the walls
in the proper sequence: head, fore-edge,
tail, then spine.

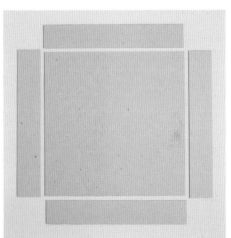

1b

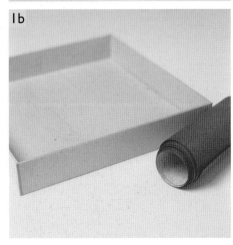

2a

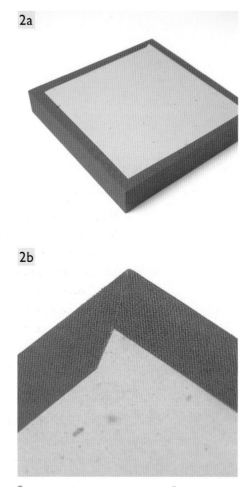

2b

2c

2a–c   COVER THE TRAY. Cut a strip of bookcloth to a measurement of twice the depth of the tray plus 1 ½" (4 cm), and long enough to wrap around all four walls plus ½" (1 cm).

2d   Cover the tray (see The Basics, page 21).

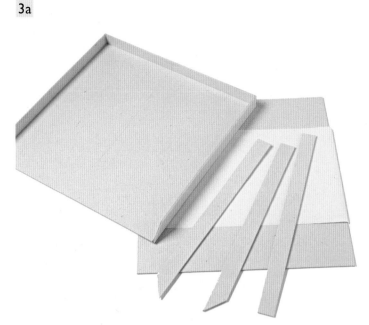

3a, b **CUT OUT THE BOARDS** for the lid, following the lay-out below. The lid is a three-walled tray, inverted over the lower tray and hinged to it at the back (head) wall. There is no head wall to the lid. Because the lid takes its measurements from the covered tray, start by squaring a piece of board (see The Basics, page 20), and placing the tray on the squared corner. Mark the board, and cut:

Base:

Height = height of tray plus two cloth thicknesses

Width = width of tray plus two cloth thicknesses

Tail wall:

Height = desired depth of lid plus one board thickness

Width = width of tray plus two cloth thicknesses (same as width of base)

Spine and fore-edge walls:

Height = height of base plus two board thicknesses

Width = desired depth of lid plus one board thickness (same as height of tail wall)

NEXT **CONSTRUCT THE LID.** Angle the ends of the spine and fore-edge walls. Glue up the tray (see The Basics, page 20), starting with the tail wall and proceeding to the spine and fore-edge walls.

3b

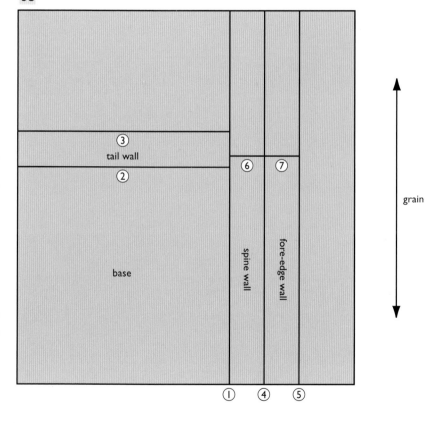

③ tail wall
②
base
⑥ spine wall
⑦ fore-edge wall
① ④ ⑤
grain

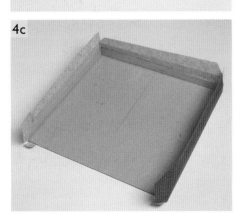

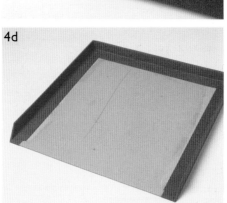

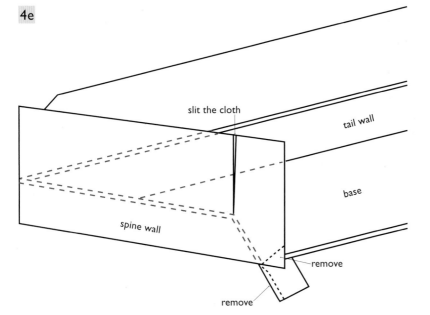

4a   COVER THE LID.

4b   Cut a strip of bookcloth to a measurement of twice the depth of the tray plus 1½" (4 cm), and long enough to wrap around all three walls plus 1½" (4 cm).

4c, d   Cover the tray, following the same procedure as for covering a four-walled tray (see The Basics, page 21). Allow a ¾" (2 cm) turn-in at the angled edges of the spine and fore-edge walls.

4e, f   Do not glue these turn-ins onto the board until the tray has been wrapped and the appropriate cuts have been made (see diagram).

slit the cloth

tail wall

base

spine wall

remove

remove

5 ATTACH THE LID TO THE TRAY.
Cut two hinge strips from the bookcloth, both to the same dimensions:
Height = 1 1/2" (4 cm)
Width = width of tray (outside)
One hinge connects the lid to the tray on the outside, at the head wall. The second hinge covers the lid-to-tray attachment on the inside.

Place the lid on the tray. Glue out one hinge. Stick it down, 3/4" (2 cm) onto the lid and centered. Press with your bone folder. Shape the cloth against the right angle formed by the lid and the head wall of the tray, and press the cloth down well, against the wall. Let the box sit closed, for 10 to 15 minutes.

Open the lid and roll the box onto its head wall. Place the second hinge (unglued) in the box, centered over the joint space between the lid and the tray. Trim slivers of cloth off each end so that the cloth fits perfectly inside the tray. Glue out this strip and stick it down. Immediately force the cloth into the joint with a bone folder. Rub vigorously until the cloth is well-adhered to all surfaces. Let the box sit open, for a few minutes, then close the box and let it sit under weights for 1/2 hour.

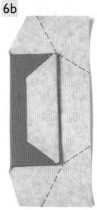

6a

6c

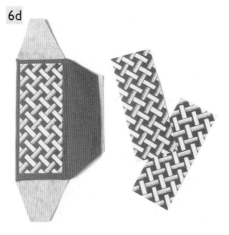

6b

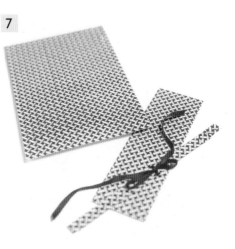

6d

7

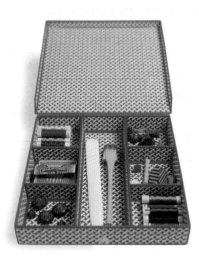

6a–d **MAKE AND ADHERE THE PARTITION WALLS.** (See the Tip on the next page)

Mark the base of the tray for their placement.

Glue out the bottom flanges of each partition and adhere the partition to the base. When the glue has begun to set, apply glue to the side flanges and press them onto the tray walls.

Note: It is easier to line the partition walls with decorative paper before gluing them into the box. In my box, the two long partitions must be lined after all of the partitions are attached in order to hide the flanges from the short partitions. All of the short partitions, however, can be covered before attaching them—and that is what I did. Depending on the configuration of your walls, you must make your own decision.

7 **LINE THE BOX.** Cut strips of decorative paper to line the lid and tray walls (inside and out). Apply adhesive and stick them down. Cut pieces of decorative paper to cover the floors of all the compartments. Apply adhesive and stick them down. Cut one piece of either paper or bookcloth to line the bottom of the box (outside). Apply adhesive and stick it down. Cut two pieces of paper to cover and line the lid. Apply adhesive to these papers and stick them down. With the box open and sitting on its head wall, press the lid by filling it with newsprint and weights. Leave for several hours, until dry.

Tip: How to Make Partition Boards

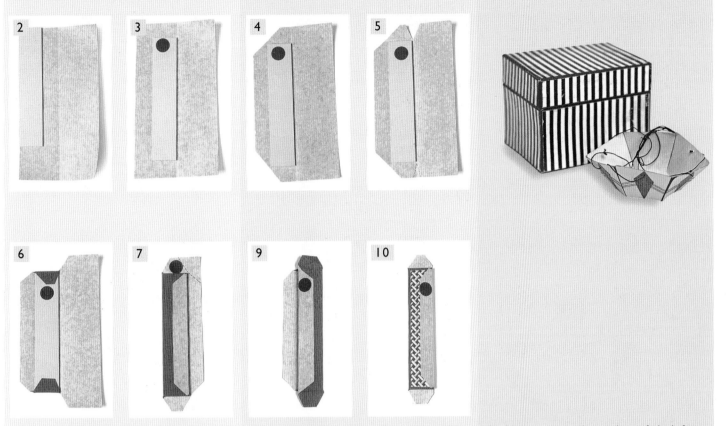

All of the four-walled projects described in this book (the Candy, Jewelry, and Letter boxes) can have partition walls built into them. Just remember that the flanges attaching the partitions to the tray should be disguised somehow. In The Ornament Box, the walls are covered with strips of decorative paper to hide the construction details. If the tray and walls are covered in a patterned paper—the busier the better—this protective coloration will help the flanges disappear into the walls. The models above illustrate the ten steps in making partitions.

1. Cut out the partitions. The boards should fit from wall to wall with a little breathing room. In depth, they should be shallower than the interior depth of the tray by one board thickness.

2. Cut out the cloth or covering paper:
Height = height of board plus 1 1/2" (4 cm)
Width = twice the width of the board plus 1 1/2" (4 cm)
Crease the cloth in half lengthwise.

3. Glue out the board and position it on the cloth against the crease mark; center it heightwise. Press.

4. Cut corners off the cloth, at the head and tail near the 3/4" (2 cm) turn-ins only. Keep cuts one-and-a-half board thicknesses away from the tips of the board.

5. Remove triangular wedges of cloth from the head and tail turn-ins, at the creased center of the bookcloth. Cut in close to the board.

6. Glue the head and tail turn-ins, bringing them onto the board and pinching in the cloth at the corners.

7. Glue out the board and roll it onto the right-hand half of the creased cloth. Press it down well.

8. Cut corners off the cloth at the head and tail.

9. Sharply fold the four cloth extensions backward, onto themselves, to form the flanges.

10. If desired, line the partitions with decorative paper. (See the Note in Step 6.)

This house of cards will never come tumbling down! Architecturally, it's a simple saltbox. Structurally, it's a handful of postcards laced together with linen thread. The charming and eccentric model for The Buttonhole Stitched Box was found by my friend Robert Warner at the famous 26th Street Flea Market in New York City. I only wish we knew who—thirty, forty, fifty years ago—gathered fourteen postcards, threaded a needle, sat down, and built a house.

the buttonhole stitched box...
memories of special flea market finds

MATERIALS	Graph paper	Fourteen postcards—	Pressure-sensitive adhesive
	Card stock	ten horizontal views	Linen thread
		and four vertical views	Ribbon

getting started:
preparing the postcards

Trim all postcards to the same size.

Divide the postcards into pairs—five horizontal and two vertical.

Apply a strip of pressure-sensitive adhesive to the center of one card of each pair, sticking the two cards together.

1

1 CUT A SHEET OF GRAPH PAPER and a piece of card stock to the same height and width as the postcards. Stick the two together with strips of pressure-sensitive adhesive.

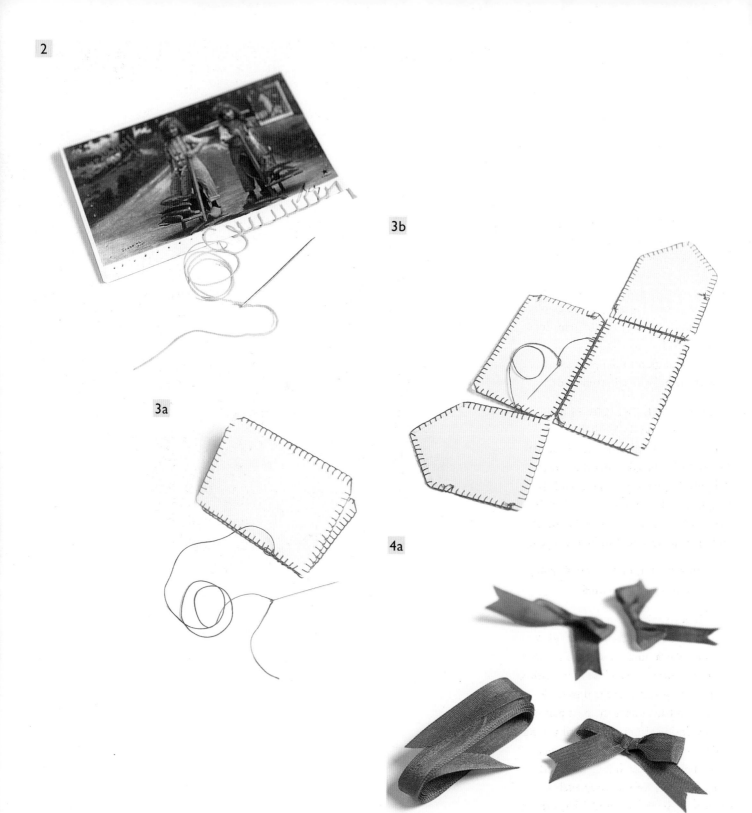

2

3b

3a

4a

NEXT   ANGLE THE TWO VERTICAL
WALLS by cutting off triangular wedges
to create a roof line.

NEXT   MAKE A PATTERN for punching holes. Using the grid on the graph
paper, punch holes at $1/4$" (0.5 cm) intervals around all four edges of this card.
Clamp the pattern to the postcards and
transfer the holes to all seven cards.

2   EMBROIDER THE EDGES of all the
cards with a buttonhole stitch.
This is a simple overcast stitch in which
the needle is slipped under the thread
and pulled up tautly as the stitch is being
completed. Move from right to left. It
doesn't matter if you start at the top of the
card or its underside. Just be consistent.

3a   LINK THE CARDS TOGETHER
with a running overcast stitch.

3b   To start, pick any two adjacent panels and hold them face-to-face. Slide a
threaded needle under the two links that
sit on the outer edges of the cards. Bring
the thread up and over the tops of the
cards, then back under the next pair of
links. Continue in this way until you have
reached the ends of the cards. Tie off
with a knot. Repeat to join all panels.
Note: Only one of the roof panels is
stitched to the vertical walls. The other is
left free and flips up to provide access to
the box.

4a, b   DECORATE THE BOX with small
ribbon bows tacked on where desired.

supply sources

ADAMS MAGNETIC PRODUCTS
2081 North 15th Avenue
Melrose Park, IL 60160
(800) 222-6686
Fax: (732) 389-8128
Magnetic strips and sheets

AIKO'S ART MATERIALS IMPORT, INC.
3347 North Clark Street
Chicago, IL 60657
(773) 404-5600
Fax: (773) 404-5919
Japanese paper; bookcloth; tools; books on
bookbinding; general art materials

AMERICAN GRAPHIC ARTS, INC.
150 Broadway
Elizabeth, NJ 07206
(908) 351-6906
Fax: (908) 351-7156
Reconditioned bookbinding equipment,
such as board shears, presses, stamping
equipment

ARISTA SURGICAL SUPPLY CO., INC.
67 Lexington Avenue
New York, NY 10010
(212) 679-3694
Fax: (212) 696-9046
Knives, handles and blades; micro-spatulas

BOOKMAKERS INTERNATIONAL LTD.
6701B Lafayette Avenue
Riverdale Park, MD 20737
(301) 927-7787
Fax: (301) 927-7715
Bookbinding supplies, equipment and
tools; books on bookbinding

CAMPBELL-LOGAN BINDERY, INC.
212 Second Street, North
Minneapolis, MN 55401-1433
(800) 942-6224
Fax: (612) 332-1313
Japanese bookcloth

DIEU DONNÉ PAPERMILL, INC.
433 Broome Street
New York, NY 10013-2622
(212) 226-0573
Fax: (212) 226-6088
Handmade paper; books

HARCOURT BINDERY
51 Melcher Street
Boston, MA 02210
(617) 542-5858
Fax: (617) 451-9058
Bookbinding supplies, equipment and tools

IRIS NEVINS DECORATIVE PAPERS
PO Box 429
Johnsonburg, NJ 07846
(908) 813-8617
Fax: (908) 813-3431
Marbling supplies, tools; marbled paper.
Reproduces historical patterns.

NEW YORK CENTRAL ART SUPPLY, INC.
62 Third Avenue
New York, NY 10003
(212) 473-7705; (800) 950-6111
Fax: (212) 475-2513
Paper of all kinds; bookcloth; books; general art materials

PAPERCONNECTION INTERNATIONAL
208 Pawtucket Avenue
Cranston, RI 02905
(401) 461-2135
Fax: (401) 331-4070
Papers, mostly Japanese handmades

TALAS
568 Broadway
New York, NY 10012-1996
(212) 219-0770
Fax: (212) 219-0735
Paper; bookbinding supplies, equipment
and tools; books

index

about the author

Barbara Mauriello is an artist and conservator who has a bookbinding studio in Hoboken, New Jersey. She teaches bookbinding and boxmaking at the International Center of Photography, The Center for Book Arts, and Penland School of Crafts.

BARBARA MAURIELLO

Women of the Bible: From Abigail to the Queen of Sheba

sixteen paper boxes within a cloth-covered folding box

remnants of an eighteenth-century fire-and-water damaged book; bookcloth over boards, Momi and dyed Japanese tissue papers; pewter clasp

9 $\frac{1}{2}$" x 9 $\frac{1}{2}$" x 2 $\frac{1}{2}$" (24 cm x 24 cm x 6 cm)